IRISH
GAME
FISHING

IRISH GAME FISHING

BY

PAUL SHEEHAN

SWAN·HILL
PRESS

First published in the UK in 1997
by Swan Hill Press,
an imprint of Airlife Publishing Ltd

British Library Cataloguing-in-Publication Data
A catalogue record for this book
is available from the British Library

ISBN 1 85310 843 X

Typeset by Phoenix Typesetting,
Ilkley, West Yorkshire.
Printed in Italy.

Swan Hill Press
an imprint of Airlife Publishing Ltd
101 Longden Road, Shrewsbury, England, SY3 9EB.

Contents

Acknowledgements

My mother bought me my first fishing rod; without her help I would not have been able to follow my instincts.

I cannot imagine angling without companionship. I am grateful to my pals down the years, Tom Keldon, Leslie Bryan (who supplied the correct forms of most Irish names in the text, and many of the literary references), Tony Cains, David Grayson, Paul Voorheis and Enda Lee for the company, the arguments, the sharing of small triumphs and disasters. The only thing worse than seeing your friend catch a salmon or a big trout is hearing about it many times afterwards; we have freely inflicted this on each other from time to time. I owe much to that expert angler Robert Gillespie. I am also indebted to Davy Campbell, Pat Cleere, Jim Doyle, Frank Elliott, Ralph Fitzjohn, Norman and Stewart Greene, Rory Harkin, Charlie Hegarty, David Hughes, Pat Hughes, Bob Hutchinson, Tim Moore, Ethna O' Brien, Tommy Simpson, Jim Stafford, Lance Thomson, John Todd, Ken Whelan, and David Wilde. Colin McKelvie helped in the outline preparation, and Veronica Morrow assisted in repairing some of the damaged language which appeared in initial drafts. I owe thanks to Roy Eaton, David Goodchild and Mark Bowler for their encouragement along the way. My thanks are also due to Sandy Leventon, John Wilshaw and EMAP Pursuit Publications for permission to base some material in this book on articles which first appeared in *Trout and Salmon*. I am particularly grateful to the Northern Ireland Tourist Board for all its assistance.

The days when Denise has fished with me have been some of my most memorable. And when she's not been there I have always looked forward to coming home to her, and to Aoife and Eoin.

Introduction

The traditional rhythms of country sports are changing. Once, there was a season for everything. To the angler this meant a time to fish, and a time to hang up his rods to let the quarry breed in peace; but that was when species were created in the course of natural evolution. Now they can be developed in the geneticist's laboratory and the idea of a close season for these seems quaint rather than functional. In certain European countries, one can fish for artificially reared and stocked trout throughout the year, or for salmon bred in cages and introduced into alien stillwaters. To me this is control of stock and environment which has gone too far. If the angler loses entirely the ancient partnership with the progress of the seasons he will lose some sense of self, of belonging to a long tradition.

Of course country sports have always involved a degree of management, of the environment, if not of the quarry. In Europe, wilderness is a relative concept and even the most remote landscapes show the mark of man, but some allow the imagination more scope than others, and these are the places where the angler finds his own space. They are not always the most distant. John Waller Hills' *A Summer on the Test* was written about Houghton club waters, where fish were fed in stews and turned into the river when they were two pounds or more in weight. This did not prevent Hills from describing, more evocatively than almost any other writer since, the nerve-charged lone pursuit, and the sense of the pastoral, which are the distinguishing experiences of angling.

The essential fact is that angling cannot be reduced to a mere game; it is a country sport whose evolving traditions both sustain the slow burn of original interest, and shape its codes of behaviour. It becomes decadent when the quarry can be converted into cash (by whatever means), or cash too easily converted into a tame quarry. I once saw a photograph of a concrete, suburban swimming pool in a far eastern city, surrounded by anglers seated at close intervals, fishing. This hellish vision is the terminus for a particular line of modern angling development which is profit-centred and tries to domesticate an instinct for the wild. However, most anglers seem to recognise this and seek to return to authentic sport in wild places.

I wanted to fish long before I saw a fish; the moment it crystallised was when, at six, I saw the running water of a little rivulet near the farm in County Laois where I spent my boyhood. To some of us this is an instinct as organic as the stirrings in the psyche roused by the onset of spring and autumn; and even hundreds of years of urban experience have not erased ancestral memories of those ancient rhythms from the modern mind. So to fish in wild places, with the grain of the sporting year, is deeply fulfilling. The Irish game angler is privileged, because this is a country where salmon, brown trout, and sea-trout, all native species, are still sought according to the cycles of the seasons.

One of the unique characteristics of Irish angling is that each stage of the angler's calendar has the quality of a popular festival. There is a collective excitement in the catchments of every spring salmon river as the opening day approaches, affecting all true salmon anglers, whatever their means. Around mid-May, anglers head west to the great limestone loughs for the mayfly season, and at this time of year Oughterard on the Corrib or Ballinrobe on Lough Mask become angling towns. By June the grilse run has begun on the Moy and it is impossible to pass through Ballina or Foxford and not notice how the event pervades the entire lives of these communities.

The greatest change in Irish angling over the past century is that many fisheries have become more accessible, and a number attract faithful British or European visitors each year. However, it takes many years to become familiar with the moods of just one water. What this book sets out to describe is the *when* of Irish fishing; the most opportune times to fish particular waters, or for particular species. I say opportune because there is rarely a right time, only periods which are more or less favourable. It also clearly reflects personal choice and experience, so what you will find here is a selection of Irish waters which give a flavour of the fishing on the island. I am conscious of those omitted, but they are usually left out because I do not know them well enough. For example I have little knowledge of the County Kerry fisheries, Lough Currane and the river Laune, so although both have justifiable reputations as splendid waters I cannot describe what I have not personally experienced.

Angling for wild fish is less predictable than fishing for, say, trout stocked in sizes and densities which the host water cannot possibly support unaided. It can also appear, superficially, less rewarding than success which is measured in limit bags, and gross weights. However, an angler who comes in off an Irish lough with a brace of two pound trout, or returns from a brawling western river with a spring salmon or a grilse, has had a contact with the very essence of his sport. If he does not value this he does not deserve it. He is also very rare because increasingly, men and women come to Ireland for the experience of a traditional angling which has been lost elsewhere.

CHAPTER ONE

Beginnings

My Irish fishing began on a trout stream and this is still, sometimes, the way I open the season. I used to take the bus from Dublin and go to Newbridge, on the middle course of the Liffey. This is not only a capital's river, it is also a very varied fishery. The lower reaches between Islandbridge and Lucan are fished for salmon. Above, almost all of it is a trout fishery. The river describes a big loop, flowing west from its beginnings in the Wicklow hills, where the trout are very small, to the middle reaches in Kildare, near Newbridge, then gradually turning east, past Clane, a mature river with deeper streams and bigger fish.

Wet-fly fishing on the Slaney.

The river at Newbridge was a fine trout stream, quick, fairly broad, flowing over a steep gradient above the town, with lots of good fast glides and lively stickles. In early spring this rough water held plenty of trout and I used to fish it down with wet-fly, and had enough takes and fish to satisfy me. But I met there one day a local angler who fished upstream, not with a conventional floating line, but a slow sinker, and the delicacy of his fishing was compelling to watch. On every Irish water there are craftsmen like this. One of the best-known fished on the Suir in Tipperary, near Holycross, a wicker creel strapped on his back, and a long, whole-bamboo rod in his strong right hand; he fished a short line, using small flies, and his signature was a rapid rhythm of cast drift, cast drift, before moving on.

My most memorable spring trouting was on the upper stretches of the Liffey, above the lake at Blessington. There, upstream of Kilbride, the little river rides over the back of the Wicklow hills. It is fed by many small brooks – Lugnalee brook, Ballylow Brook – but remains a shallow stream, with low banks and a gravel bottom easily waded. It was full of trout. The fishing was simple and remains so. A soft rod, perhaps ten feet long, a short line, and a team of three small wet-flies were all you needed. You could have used any tackle from the past one hundred years and it would not have affected your presentation or your pleasure a whit. The most delicate fishing was done by flicking out just so much line that the cast alone settled in the water, and drifted for a few yards before it came around below you. On a crisp Good Friday in early April many years ago, a friend and myself fished down a couple of miles of water like this, taking over a dozen trout each. That day stays in the mind in particular because of the crystal brightness of the spring air between showers, and the keen wind on the highlands. We warmed ourselves by chasing a mink, at that time a novelty, which brazenly loitered on the riverbank.

All of the advances in materials and techniques have made little impression on this fishing; that angler of the Suir was one of the best in the district, and he would still have been so with a rod of hazel cut from a hedgerow, as described in the earliest fishing book in the English language, the *Treatyse of Fysshynge wyth an Angle*. Modern materials, gadgetry, fancy theories, can cloud the truth, most evident in the simplicity of early spring trouting, but applicable to all angling, that it is the mind fully engaged in the pursuit, and the hand practised to do the mind's bidding with unconscious skill, which connect act and instinct.

* * *

The most successful Irish anglers I know possess a quality of casual but deadly skill. Robbie O' Grady of Ballinrobe is a first-rate lough fisherman, still getting all his trout by a method standard not just for decades but for centuries. He will entertain you with story and song while fishing his flies with uncommon command. We have always cherished the cult of the amateur in Ireland, and this, along with a native cuteness which is sharpened almost to cynicism by daily life in small communities, where everyone knows everything about everyone else, is perhaps why we have been spared the fads of consumer angling – meretricious expertise, stockpond trophyism, and all the rest. Long may it remain so.

The spirit of Irish fishing has not changed much, but the fishing itself has altered in the last decades of this century. We still fish, in the main, for native wild fish, though there is some stocking of brown trout on certain loughs, but brown trout fishing is probably more variable now than for some time past.

Fishing on some of the western limestone loughs has become more difficult. It is uncertain whether this is part of a cyclical pattern or something worse. Studies have verified eutrophic change, due to enrichment from agricultural and urban effluents in Lough Conn. There are already consequences: algal blooms have been seen on the lough, and the average weight of trout is increasing. Conn trout were noted for being free-rising – but are less so nowadays. There is also a query about disimproving water quality on Mask. But it is worth remarking here that almost every book written about Irish fishing for at least a hundred years has said that the western loughs are going to the bad. Francis Francis said so after fishing Conn in 1873: 'it is only a pity that trout are not more plentiful in the lough, as half-a-dozen in the day is a good take' (*Angling Reminiscences*, 1887. *A Month in the West*). T.C. Kingsmill-Moore wrote that the great days of the Corrib were over before he started to fish it in 1926, and that it had been in decline since the turn of the century. 'I fished the lake for ten years and in that time it had deteriorated so much that I sought other waters. Now I am told it is beginning to improve again, but a few days trial in 1960 was disappointing' (*A Man May Fish*, 1960). A.A. Luce knew Mask and Conn very well; his chapters on them in *Fishing and Thinking* (1959), are the best writing about these loughs ever. He also thought that they were then declining and agreed with the pessimists whose '. . . general impression is that these lakes "went off" catastrophically some twenty or more years ago'.

However, the evidence of environmental change in Conn especially is scientifically well-grounded and must be believed, and recent stock surveys on Lough Mask show a reduction in trout numbers and an increase in pike. What is certain is that these loughs are part of the national heritage, and I would see the Liffey dry up before I would let them become mere boating lakes. They still provide splendid sport on their day; the 1996 mayfly season on Corrib was one of the best in recent years. To be afloat on them, with fish rising, is one of the great experiences of Irish angling.

The larger rivers are recovering from the arterial drainage schemes of the 1950s and 1960s, which forever changed the character of the Moy and the Boyne, for example. The trout have returned, however, and the Boyne is now producing trout as big as ever. This holds for many other dredged rivers. The shame is that the widened riverbeds require more maintenance than formerly, but the fish are there, big fish in the case of the Boyne, which regularly yields six, seven, and eight-pounders to the dry-fly.

The modern agents of change have particularly affected the habitat of brown trout. Intensive agricultural practices were introduced without thought for the consequences. Big pig-rearing units produced vast quantities of slurry which were allowed to run into river courses and loughs. This almost killed Lough Sheelin. Highly toxic run-off from silage pits caused fish kills in low summer levels in streams. Effluents from growing towns have combined with enriched run-off from artificially fertilised land to cause algal blooms in some waters, even to the

11

extent of affecting Lough Conn. Peat silt has affected Lough Derg; and excessive numbers of sheep on western hills has produced overgrazing and deposition of peat silt in local loughs.

Some of the acute problems mentioned have been tackled. Legislation and advice have both greatly reduced pollution from silage effluents. Some urban pollution, like that of Mullingar which temporarily stopped the fishing in Lough Ennell, has been addressed, and in that case so successfully that Ennell is once again a clean, productive fishery. In recent years, Sheelin has produced magnificent sport with huge brown trout taking mayfly which have returned to hatch in massive quantities.

The case of the sea-trout is instructive. Populations of sea-trout in certain parts of the west almost disappeared, after a catastrophic decline in the late 1980s. The decline coincided with the operation of inshore fish farms in many of the affected areas. Some angling interests blamed the fish farms, which denied liability, claiming lack of scientific proof. However, the government commissioned a study which concluded that it would be wise to introduce a fallowing system on the fish farms. This would destroy the concentrations of sea-lice which were generated around the cages, and which were held responsible by some for the disappearance of the sea-trout. The early signs are encouraging, and there is a delicate revival of sea-trout in some of the affected areas.

Salmon fishing is very good. Spring fishing is scarce, but then so it is everywhere in northern Europe, and Irish fishing is much more accessible than most. Summer salmon and grilse fishing is phenomenally good. The Moy and the Foyle systems produce thousands of fish each. I know of a chap who had thirty-eight grilse in a day on a County Donegal river in 1995. My friend Robert Gillespie has often taken ten or more in a day from the Moy, and in recent years would average about one hundred fish a season. Even the little rivers offer superlative fishing on their day – last year a small spate stream in south Donegal produced nine grilse in a day, on the fly, to an acquaintance of mine. And by the way, that was free fishing.

A great advance is that inland fishery management in Ireland is better than it has ever been. The agency largely responsible for this was the Inland Fisheries Trust, now the Central Fisheries Board (CFB), and the regional fisheries boards. The Trust did a brilliant job of scientific investigation, protection and promotion, and every angler who fishes in Ireland owes its staff a debt, sometimes unacknowledged.

The Trust, later the CFB, also began the state management of fisheries, and these – for example the Erriff – are shining examples of how a fishery should be run, and of how the range of state resources are essential to the nurture of such places. The Erriff was a beautiful river in a lovely valley which produced between two and three hundred salmon a year before the Board took it over. Inland poaching was stopped by fisheries staff; marine control over excessive netting was established; redds were created. Now the river produces eight hundred fish a year and attracts visitors from far and wide.

Private owners have done their bit too, and the staff at Screebe, Peter Mantle, who has revived Delphi, and Ralph Fitzjohn, assisted by Tim Moore, who have poured effort into rebuilding Costello and Fermoyle fishery, demonstrate that capital and vigorous management is needed if these fisheries are to retain their stock, and their character.

It has taken the goads of pollution and over-exploitation to make us realise the wealth of this heritage; and it has taken time to acknowledge that though it may be owned by individuals, there is a community of interest involved. In times past, the local poached because he was not allowed to fish, under any circumstances. When the landlords left, a residual grudge against private fishing rights was freely translated into a general belief in free access for all, but we are coming to see the necessity for strong ownership. Free access meant no responsibility. Now the good proprietor, whether the state or an individual, is preserving a traditional environment and making it open to all for a fairly modest sum. I felt a glow of national pride at Burrishoole one day, when two Scots proprietors, from a renowned river in the highlands, arrived on a visit expressly to see how the fishery, run by the state-sponsored Salmon Research Agency, was managed.

So we have progressed, and the Irish angler is no longer the loner of old. Many of us belong to angling organisations, both local and national. Before my optimism runs away with me, I will mention a piece of Brendan Behan apocrypha, which has it that the first item on the agenda of many Irish organisations is The Split. We are just getting over the effects, especially on the

River Drowes. Estuary Pools and Donegal Bay.

western loughs, of the rod licence dispute, when, in a controversy over a proposed national rod licence, some anglers would have no fishing on the loughs, while others insisted on their right to do so. Whatever the merits of either case, the short-term effects on the loughs were not good, and everyone has suffered the consequences. A noted Irish parliamentarian once famously asked 'Why should we do anything for posterity? What has posterity ever done for us': there will always be a lurking sympathy here for this sentiment.

But the fishing is still marvellous. The loughs, big and small, can be magical. Take Lough Carra, there is no stillwater in these islands like it, with water so clear over white sands that fishing it is like fishing in a tropical lagoon. And every river in Ireland has its brown trout. Last year in April I fished the little White Horse river near Mountrath in County Laois, which I used to look at as a boy on my way to Sunday Mass in the 1950s, and which is unknown to anyone outside the town. It was much the same, and still full of willing fish; my cousin James had a two-pounder from it not long afterwards. There are times of the year, especially in the months of May, June, and July, when there is so much good fishing that choice is difficult. Despite the ups and downs over the course of the last few decades, fishing in Ireland retains much of its richness and its wild character. The Irish angler lives among a bounty unknown in many other parts of Europe.

*   *   *

The salmon angler in Ireland in the last decade of this century is particularly fortunate. He can start very early in the year, with real hopes of getting a fish, and he can reasonably expect fish in every month up to, and including October. In the months of the grilse run he can enjoy sport equal to any this century.

I am concerned here with the angler at the very beginning of the year, on the first of January. He can start on the Liffey and, within sight of the capital's low skyline, land a January springer at Islandbridge. I have friends who have done so – Stephen Buchanan has landed some beautiful Liffey springers here – but it is a hard grind and often whole weeks go by without word of a fish. I have an ambition to take a Liffey springer, but it will have to wait until my retirement, when I can invest the necessary days and weeks.

No, not the Liffey, but the Drowes, in Counties Donegal and Leitrim, is the best place to be in January. This is a glorious little river, only five miles long from its source in Lough Melvin, to the sea, where it runs over shingle into Donegal Bay. It is a jaunty, lively stream for almost the whole of its course, and its proportions allow the most delicate fly-fishing for early season salmon. They are caught in reasonable numbers, averaging perhaps forty or more fish a month from January to April, then the run of grilse, which is very early on this river, swells the take, which most seasons amounts to well over one thousand fish. Often a fish is taken on opening day, the first of January. They usually star in the national press on the next day, and Bill Likely's fishery office at Lareen, at the head of the river, has its walls covered with press pictures of the first salmon in each of many seasons. There are lots of images there to whet the appetite, notably one of two fish, weighing twenty-eight pounds and seventeen pounds, taken in one day by an angler fishing the Sea Pool. The average fish are smaller, of course, at about nine pounds, but they are as fresh as you are likely to find, having run no distance from the sea. And almost every week big double-figure fish, in the teens or twenties of pounds, are got, though how they are landed on this rocky shallow river must often be a mystery.

The Drowes flows in the shadow of Ben Bulben, whose great edge jutting towards the Atlantic, like a ship's prow, often seems to be in peripheral vision as you fish the river. It is prominent at the estuary, where the road bridge marks the limit of the tidal influence. Downstream are the Estuary Pools, a series of connected pools, constructed in 1995 to replace the traps formerly there. The top pool is the favourite, perhaps because in the grilse season fish lie here in thick shoals before hazarding the shallows just upstream of the bridge, and the angler sees these first as he crosses the bridge before beginning to fish. The other pools in the series also hold fish, but again, mainly grilse. There is a feeling that springers do not like to lie here and run straight through. Whatever the season, fishing here, with Donegal Bay open before you just beyond the shingle, and the rhythm of the breakers in your ears, is like fishing in the ocean.

The Sea Pool is just above the bridge. This is really a length of water rather than a single pool, which is of note because sea-liced fish often choose to lie here. The water is flat and needs a wind to roughen it into good fishing trim, especially for the fly, and even then the fly must be helped by hand draws in normal water heights. This is a deadly place for a big spring fish on a spring tide, and it is said that you should be fishing about an hour or two before the ebb begins.

The river above divides into two sections. Upstream of the Four Masters' bridge, almost as far as the outflow from Melvin, is a wonderful stretch of fly water, created by the most judicious use of weirs and groynes, and accessible for all its length because the river is bordered by a walkway of wooden planking. The pools on this are a joy to fish, some of them, like the Tinkers Pool and the pools just below, offering some of the finest spring salmon fly-fishing in Ireland. It is also unusual in that most regulars fish with single-handed rods and light, slow-sinking lines, rated at six or seven, with a size six or eight shrimp fly at the business end. Peter McSharry, who took me along the river on my first day, used this tackle to land two spring fish of ten pounds each on a February day in 1995. When I first fished it, I did so with a fifteen foot rod and number eleven fast sink and sink tip lines, which is my standard gear for cold-water springers, but was far too much gun for this river. Still, I feel that a longish rod has advantages even here and a grilse rod of thirteen foot, paired with a number seven or eight sink-tip line, would be a handy combination.

The last few pools on this stretch are first-rate spring pools. The Crooked Pool was one of the best on the river until the Mill Pool was built. The river sweeps into it after a sharp and a bend, and the water velocity has scooped out good lies behind rocks. Nature has been assisted by a small weir, so that the main flow lies against the left bank, from where one usually fishes, and across which a fly can be led on an easy leash. One feels a fish could lie, and take, anywhere here. This stream discharges into a smallish pool before flowing into the Mill Pool, really excellent holding water, some one hundred yards long. It has produced many big salmon.

15

A *fresh-run February springer*.

Below the Four Masters' bridge are a couple of newly created pools, and then a long slow reach, which speeds up again into fast water before Lennox's bridge. For about half a mile upstream, and a little longer downstream, as far as the Perch Pool, is lovely fly water, all of it capable of producing fish. I was first told about the excellence of this stretch by a Donegal angler, who had taken a fresh thirteen-pound fish, on fly, from the flat by the first telegraph pole, just below Lennox's bridge, during the last week in February.

Below the Perch Pool, down to the Muddy Pool and beyond, is flat, fairly deep water, and though usually more of interest to the bait angler than the fly angler, it can produce good spring fish to the knowledgable fly-fisher. The slow water does not deter Drowes regulars, many of whom fish bait from the first day. The river allows all methods, and is open along its entire length to day ticket anglers, from opening day on the first of January until about mid-March. From then on, anglers who take the cottages at Lareen, which are let by the week, have exclusive rights to the river above Four Masters' bridge.

The river is heavily fished at weekends throughout the year, and there are many anglers even on weekdays during the grilse run. There is no beat system and no limit on the number of rods. This can be uncomfortable when a fish shows in front of you and a shrimp fisher is loitering nearby; then his float will zip into the water at your feet, and he will edge ever closer. If you turn away to free a trapped fly, he will be standing where you just stood. You cannot afford to move any distance from the water because you will lose your place, which is all very disagreeable. The answer is to fish at midweek in early spring, when you can have splendid fishing on miles of river, with plenty of room for everyone.

The grilse fishing is also very good, with huge numbers of fish running the river. There is no registration system, and many anglers go off at the end of the day without reporting their bag, so the size of the annual take is uncertain, though it is substantial. There is heavy traffic both in the stream and on the banks at this time of year, and with unlimited numbers of anglers, things can get too crowded for me. I prefer to fish the Estuary Pools at this time; fishing is available on a day ticket for a modest sum, and between eight o' clock in the morning and six in the evening one can fish for the hundreds of grilse which sometimes lie in these pools. Fishing is limited to eight rods per day. The grilse run is early here, with the main surges of fish coming through at the end of May and the beginning of June. They really are bonny fish, with the bloom of the sea still on their flanks. If you can ignore the caravan park on the left bank, a relic of 1960s taste, you may fish for grilse as they come in off the tides, in racing pools sided by shingle banks, with the salt spray of Donegal Bay gusting in your face.

CHAPTER 2

Spring Trout and the Duckfly

For many trout anglers the year begins on the loughs, with the duckfly season. The duckfly is a general name for chironomids or buzzers, and no particular species is intended. Rather it covers any of the chironomids which can hatch heavily in the early months of the year, and bring fish to the surface in loughs as different as Corrib and Owel. The duckfly season can be very early; sometimes there is very good fishing in late February. As a rule the weeks between mid-March and mid-April cover the peak of hatches, and if my life depended on picking one week it would be the last week in March. However, as I will explain later, I would never gamble anything of importance on getting the timing of a duckfly hatch right.

Anglers might reasonably object that this is too early to be fishing for wild brown trout, which will only just be getting over the hardships of winter, and the effects of spawning. They need quiet in these early months to put on weight and regain condition. Some of us will have had the experience of catching April trout which felt like dishcloths and squirted milt or eggs when handled, an unpleasant experience at any time, but especially in a boat on a windswept lough on a cold day. However, Corrib trout taking the duckfly are usually in nice condition and a pleasure to see after the winter. Many of these will not have spawned, and will have fed on molluscs through the dark months. (It is thought that Corrib trout spawn only every second year). So there is nothing unsporting in braving the rigours of March or April weather on a big lough to entice one of these lovely trout. Similarly, many Lough Owel trout will have wintered well and will be in good condition, but things are a little different here, and one will need to avoid shoals of small stockfish introduced at the beginning of the season, to get authentic sport with wild or grown-on fish.

J. R. Harris was one of the first angler entomologists to realise the significance of chironomids. His *An Angler's Entomology* was published in 1952 and is one of the finest and most influential Irish angling books of this century. It was the angler's entomology for these islands for many years, and it remains a sound source of reference for the whole area. Because its findings were based largely on experiences of Irish waters, it is indispensable for the trout fisher in Ireland and it will continue to be a point of reference until someone with a similarly wide experience, and skill in systematic enquiry, rolls up his sleeves.

'Dick' Harris knew and fished with the best anglers of his day. He gets honourable mentions in N. K. Robertson's *Thrifty Salmon Fishing,* and Kingsmill Moore's *A Man May Fish.* He fished a fly all over Ireland and was a deadly hunter for both trout and salmon. He was a partner in Garnett and Keegan's, a lovely fishing tackle shop in Dublin's Parliament Street, which must have given the most distinguished service anywhere in these islands. You might buy your flies from Harris, or from Mosely, another partner in the firm, both expert entomologists who combined imagination and an academic rigour, and developed some fine patterns, of which Mosely's May is outstanding. I met Harris in there, though not Mosely. A friend told me that he used to approach the counter feeling like a student going before a very exacting lecturer, terrified that he was going to say, or ask for, the wrong thing. The atmosphere of the shop, with its fine oak counters, displays of vintage reels and cased fish, and the spaciousness of another age, lingers with all those who experienced it. Both Harris and Mosely are now gone, as is the name, but there is continuity because Pat Cleere, who worked with Harris in Garnett and Keegan's, now has his own premises in Chatham Street, just off the Liffey Quays.

Brown trout from Lough Corrib.

Harris remarked on the spring rise to chironomids on Irish waters. He noticed some important features of these hatches, particularly how they tended to be localised, and consequently concentrated the trout so that they behaved, or at least clustered, as in shoals. He found that dark wet-flies, not particularly imitative, presented in the traditional way in front of a drifting boat would take trout whose attention was fixed on suspended pupae or emerging fly. But he devised a pupal pattern which would deceive fish when the wet-fly failed. He spotted how egg-laying adults would stick together and run over the water like little balls of down, and how trout refused dressings of individuals but gulped down patterns (one later christened the balling buzzer) which resembled these little clumps.

*   *   *

This is the first opportunity of the year for the boat angler to refresh his skills after the long winter lay-off. Fly-fishing from a boat on a big lough is the staple of Irish trout angling. Although many anglers fish the rivers, I would guess that many more regularly fish the loughs. It has been so for generations. Unfortunately there is little literary evidence for the way that our predecessors caught their fish, but there are many fly patterns, and actual flies, remaining, and these tell us that the methods of lough fishing have changed little in hundreds of years.

The best evidence I know is provided, appropriately, by Harris. Facing page 140 of *An Angler's Entomology* are two plates showing old Irish tyings, authenticated by Harris. They are mostly from the period 1790 to 1850, that is, about two hundred years old. The patterns for the midland loughs, and those tied by Cornelius Gorman for Loughs Mask and Inchiquin, are quite similar in construction to wet flies of today. (A similar set of flies, also tied by Cornelius Gorman, in 1791, appears in a more detailed coloured photograph opposite page viii of the Fly-fisher's Classic Library 1993 edition of James O' Gorman's *The Practice of Angling*.) They have a sloped wing, a body hackle but no throat hackle, and the body material is dubbing well picked out. They would have fished nicely just on or under the surface, and made a good disturbance as they were bobbed through the waves at the end of the cast.

Now as to the fishing of these flies, it is almost certain that they would have been fished on a short line. The first casting lines such as we know them, that is oil dressed silk lines, tapered and heavy enough to be cut through a wind, were not developed until the last quarter of the nineteenth century, and were the specific means of delivering a dry-fly on the southern English chalkstreams. The Irish angler on the loughs would have been using lines of plaited hair or silk at the times these flies were dressed, and this meant that he had to harness the wind; he could not fight it because the lines were so light, so he probably fished a short line, not much more than the length of his rod, downwind from a drifting boat. In other words, he fished much as lough fishers using the traditional approach fish today. This can be inferred from one of the reliable descriptions of contemporary angling, by O' Gorman in *The Practice of Angling*, (1845), who says of the trout in County Clare loughs,

'In stormy days they rose well at small gaudy salmon flies, but chiefly at the dropper, which we always kept skimming the wave' (Chapter XIV). O' Gorman did a lot of cross-lining on loughs, but he also fished the flies by conventional casting, especially in the evenings.

This method of fishing is easy to describe, but the subtleties of execution are impossible to appreciate except by watching a master in action. It is the most under-estimated of methods. The best wet-fly angler I know is Robbie O' Grady of Ballinrobe, who fishes Lough Mask. He uses an eleven foot rod, a model which would be a wrist breaker for me, but he is a stocky strong man with the forearms of a heavyweight, and he wields this long rod with total control throughout a fishing day. He runs a neutral density or slow sinking line through its rings, and the last time I fished with him, the line was level tapered; this is unusual, but the taper is a matter of indifference to him because he casts so little of it. He secures twelve feet or so of nylon to the end of this, almost always six pounds test. He has no time for anglers from heavily fished rainbow trout waters in England who affect two or three pound test leaders, ostensibly to rise more fish, but actually to lose whatever they hook. Three flies are attached at roughly equal intervals. He is very fussy about flies, which must be dressed in the traditional manner with plenty of hackle, and a rough body. Usually, his flies are quite big, size tens at least.

He casts a fixed length of line, about thirty feet, and as soon as it lands he begins to raise the rod, so that the flies are actually worked very little from the hand. He draws them up, very smoothly, with the long rod, so that first the bob and then the second fly are working in the most deadly taking plane for the wet-fly, the very skin of the water. He can manage a very long draw before he lifts off into another cast. He draws the flies back to him through the wave. Unlike other wet-fly anglers, he does not often cast to the side so that, especially in a big wind, the line billows like a spinnaker, and pulls the fly across the wave parallel to the front of the boat. He concentrates intensely, and manages his tackle with perfect control even in the very big winds which sweep Mask. He sees many takes which other anglers miss, and strikes a fish almost instinctively. He can fish as the centre rod on a boat, with an angler either side, and see fish come to the other flies which his companions have missed.

This is skill of a very high order, and demonstrates why the traditional wet-fly, fished in front of a drifting boat on a short line, is still the most widely favoured, and in the right hands the most deadly, way of taking brown trout from the big loughs. It can be supplemented by variations, and by other methods, but it is the foundation skill of the Irish lough angler, and the basic method for duckfly fishing, as for other hatches, during the season.

Safety is a concern on the western loughs, especially in the cold waters of the early season. They are massive, open and rocky, and are as changeable as the western skyscapes. When I first fished them the typical fishing boat was a sturdy clinker-built craft, eighteen feet or more long and broad in the beam. These were particularly stable boats in a big wave. Now fibreglass has almost taken over, and I find extra care needs to be taken in such boats, because they toss about on rough water. It is essential to have the help of a local boatman when you are new to a particular part of a lough. And you will find that almost all of them now wear some kind of floatation aid or lifejacket, and so should you. It is risky to travel too far on a lough, and especially to cross unsheltered water. Many recent fatalities have happened when anglers went afloat in a calm, and cruised too far to make their way home safely when the wind got up. It is an iron rule on the lough that even on the calmest morning a big wind will be lurking not far over the western hills. The best introduction to the western lakes is the chapter of that name in A.A. Luce's *Fishing and Thinking*. This was published in 1959, but the description of the moods of these waters (he described Conn, which he knew best), and of boatcraft, have not been surpassed and are required reading for anyone new to them.

*   *   *

The duckfly on the western loughs has for decades been associated with Corrib, although similar hatches occur elsewhere, and certainly on Carra and Mask. The fishing depends almost entirely on this hatch, and if the fly do not appear then the trout stay down. The hatch is very unpredictable, and its relationship with environmental conditions complex. I have heard it said that the best duckfly fishing follows hard winters, because the hatch is concentrated into a few short weeks, rather than dribbling out over a couple of months. Certainly in some seasons following mild winters the fishing was poor. For example, the winter of 1989 was very mild (there was virtually no frost around the Corrib), and it was wet, raising lough levels to five feet above normal. Almost all fly hatches in the following season were poor, the duckfly especially so. However, it is possible that the wrong seasons are matched in such comparisons, and, as with the mayfly, the season of egg-laying, and the season of emergence, whenever it occurs, are what should be compared.

The fly hatch around midday, and the biggest numbers appear in relatively calm conditions. They can be all sizes and colours, though they are predominantly dark. From the angling point of view the best hatches are those of biggish flies, though I have seen huge hatches of very small chironomids, in Salthouse Bay on the northern Corrib, bring fish well on the feed. Ovipositing fly can sometimes produce good fishing, but at different times. Rises to these occur at dusk, or in the early morning, provided that the weather is fairly calm.

Chironomid larvae are found all over Lough Corrib, but within specific zones. They are burrowers, and require a silty or muddy bottom, or one composed of decaying vegetable matter. Generally they hatch out in deeper water but not always so. It is the nature of the bottom, rather than the depth, which is important. When you find the right kind of ground you will find the fly, and at the right time, rising fish. The main areas are around Portcarron, near Oughterard, along the Glann shore, the water north of the Dooras peninsula (the North Lake), east of Ashford castle, especially around Salthouse Bay, and Greenfields on the eastern shore. Some of these places, for example Salthouse bay, are quite shallow. I prefer the western Corrib – Portcarron and Dooras – because there is usually shelter to be found, on the windward shore, or in the lee of islands, and the quiet water so necessary for this fishing.

23

Once you get to the general area the real problem of finding the good ground begins. Duckfly hatches can be quite localised, and concentrate the fish. It has been observed of the Dooras water that of all its hundreds of acres, only about twenty are good for the duckfly. On the other hand, in Salthouse Bay on the northern Corrib the bottom is generally silty and flush hatches of fly can occur anywhere in the bay itself.

Weather affects the fishing as well as the hatch. This is what makes duckfly angling so chancy. I have fished the duckfly in warm calms, blustery westerlies, and cold – very cold – northerlies. Sometimes only a day has separated them. For me the worst winds are from points north. These rake the entire Corrib, they are cold and it is difficult to find shelter from them. Very strong westerlies which put a shiver in the wave can be as bad. I think the most propitious conditions are a soft ripple on the water and high thin clouds above. A flat calm offers good hatching conditions but if the fish are cruising they can be impossible to approach or tempt, although they can easily be seen. But you will not often get what you want in early spring, which makes this timing one of the most difficult of the angling year. In fact I think that it is the most difficult, and I have never quite got it right, although I have usually managed to find one reasonable fishing day on my trips. I remember many more where I was out under louring skies and a black piercing wind, or on the lough in that bright glittering light, when the clouds scud overhead and a north westerly wind chills to the bone, good for walking, but not for lough fishing.

*   *   *

Most local rods fish the traditional short line even this early in the season. There are angling competitions from late February, usually in the Greenhills area, and very few of the competitors will not be fishing the short line in the approved traditional style. There are good reasons for it when conditions are right. A warmish wind and a low wave can bring on a hatch and fish will then take the traditional flies well. Some dressings are ideal for this fishing – the Blae and Black, the Sooty Olive, the Connemara Black, the Black Pennell – in small sizes.

However, conditions are so changeable at this time of year, and the fish's response to the fly so specific, that other methods are taking hold. Nowadays, anglers are getting the best out of duckfly fishing by adapting tactics developed for calm water. As much hatching and taking activity can occur in the lee of islands and sheltered bays, flies worked quietly, nymph fashion, in or near the surface, can do very well. I use either pupae patterns, or sparsely dressed wet flies, such as the Bibio, for this.

In fact a friend of mine, Neville McConnell, who fishes off Dooras, does very well with Pheasant Tails nymphs, fished slowly in this way. I was on the lough one Easter Sunday some years ago, and I went around the little piers and jetties on the northern shore, seeing how the boats were doing. Very few fish were coming in and the general feeling was that the hatch was poor. Neville told me later that he had four trout, of about two pounds each, that afternoon, fishing his little nymph slowly in the

Playing a trout on Lough Owel, April.

calm waters around the islands just off Dooras.

In such places, if you are fortunate, you can actually cast to taking fish cruising along regular routes. More usually, you will be fishing to trout which show often and move about with maddening unpredictability. As they swim near the surface their dorsals and tails cleave the water, or wiggle when they turn to gorge on suspended pupae. In a sparse hatch, it is often difficult to get near such fish without putting them down. The canny angler may find a drift line around the margin of an island where the fly is channelled and the trouts' movements are more predictable. But even if you do put a fly to the fish, it may not tempt them. They move from taking ascending pupae, to suspended pupae, to mature adults, at whim.

When trout are not showing it may be time to use a sinking line, and either wet-flies or nymphs, and experiment in fishing the team at various depths, and different speeds of retrieve. I do this as a last resort, as I am not fond of sinking lines.

The duckfly angler on Corrib must then be something of an opportunist, to profit from usually variable conditions. The long lough rod will be good for wet-fly fishing on a drift, but not for the more precise tactics in calmer water. For this a nine or ten foot rod is better, so a good compromise is a crisp ten or ten and a half foot rod, which can at a pinch fish wet-flies on a drift but also cast a nymph or pupa accurately to a spotted fish.

*   *   *

Duckfly fishing on the midland loughs can also be good. Lough Owel is best known for it and can produce remarkable fishing at times. About ten years ago, a couple of my friends fished the lough in March, with a cool northerly breeze stirring the water, and caught twenty-four trout between them. Now some of these were recently stocked fish, but many were wild or grown-on trout, and easily distinguished from the recent introductions. I fished there a few days later, on a warm breezy day with pale blue gaps in the clouds. Though we were on the water at ten there was little to cast for until noon, when the first black midges appeared and the trout came up with them. Throughout the day, but especially during the heaviest emergence in early afternoon, the rise followed this rhythm: a sudden hatch, the trout immediately boiling at fly, a sustained rise for a period, and then a pause. All of this was quite localised, and large areas of water seemed barren.

We short-lined because it perfectly suited the behaviour of the trout. They were coming at the insects just as they hatched. A size fourteen black fly, with a turn or two of soft black hackle, brushed just over the ripple, provoked rise after rise. I had a pupa representation on the point but that day the fish only saw the emerging fly.

Some weeks later, in mid-April, there was a perceptible change in the hatches and in the fishs' response to them. The fly appeared more consistently through the day, and the average size of the species was smaller. Now a pupa pattern, fished very slowly or simply allowed to drift inert in the wave, succeeded. Of course, fish still came to the bobbed fly, but it was noticeable that the point fly, as long as it was an appropriately small pupa, got the better results.

The next time out I fished a single pupa from an anchored boat just off Brown's Island. And on my first cast a trout came head and tail to the fly and the line snapped tight to the rod tip. But it was a false start. We drifted around for the next few hours without seeing a fish. At midday we approached a bank of reeds growing in six feet of water in the Bog Lakes, sheltering a small bay between a spit of land and themselves. A group of fish rose sporadically in this barely rippled, transparent water. As I carefully let down our anchor, I saw a shoal of perch six feet below sway away from the shadow of the boat. We fished about twenty yards from the rises. I suppose you can sustain the excitement of an imminent take for a little time, but if at the end you are still waiting for something to happen, the experience becomes either frustrating or interesting, according to your temperament.

An intermittent hatch of small midge came off in the bay. We tried pupae first, but they gave a poor return. In about thirty casts I had one fish come at the fly, indecisively. We changed sizes up and down, and we changed colour. We greased the leader and we proofed the pupae with floatant so that they lay in the surface film. Then I sat down to look at things a little more closely, and I became convinced that many of the fish were taking adult winged fly. Some were still intent on the pupae but I gave up on these.

So I tried dry-flies for a while. It was possible to cast into the vicinity of a rise and to be sure in that pellucid water that the fly could be seen. Still I had no offer to the artificial fly in a further half hour's fishing. Then, as I pulled in line before lifting off for a re-cast, a fish dashed at the fly, with a slash rather than a swirl. I cast again and retrieved the fly in the manner of a skated sedge. That was not the answer. Finally I cast to the rings of a rise, gave the fly a twitch and let it sit. It was taken in seconds, and I made the first decisive contact of the session. The fish actually came off after a minute's play – it is hard to avoid mishaps with a number sixteen hook, but the lock had been picked. I hooked several more fish on the small dry-fly, twitched so as to leave a tiny trail in the sheer surface. If a fish came, it was always after the movement and it was always with purpose.

When the rise failed here we moved into exposed rippled water and presently saw flat patches in the wave which indicated trout at work. The small fly was quite difficult to see, but it was not really necessary because the same tactic of a twitch and sit provoked a boil in the water visible for tens of yards. Other anglers in the area were getting sport with wet-flies, so the trout were not totally preoccupied with the adult midge. Nevertheless, it was productive to fish the dry-fly here, and it had been absolutely necessary in the calm water.

When I got home I was keen to read what Harris had said about it – well, he had been there before. On page 176 he notes that one can have interesting fishing with the dry-fly when adults linger on the surface in calm corners of the lake. And in relation to the clumps of ovipositing naturals mentioned earlier, he says that the effectiveness of the artificial is increased if 'dragged slightly on the water when a rising fish is approaching'.

27

CHAPTER 3

Slaney Springers

For more than fifteen years, in the dark morning of the appointed day of each week in early spring, I have turned my car south towards the river Slaney, and a day's salmon fishing. I cross Dublin, make my way through the western glens of the Wicklow hills, past Baltinglass and its narrow bridge by the mill, where I get my first sight of the upper river, and then continue on along narrow roads between high hedges to Bunclody in County Wexford.

The first time I did this was on St Patrick's day, 17 March 1982, when I fished with my friend Tony Cains, both of us guests of professor John Luce, a son of A. A. Luce. The Slaney was running full that day, and had a smoky grey colour reflecting the dark sky. Our right bank was open to a raw spring wind which cut to the bone. We were both spinning with Devon minnows, Tony down towards the Paling Flat, and myself in the rocky run above the Horses Head. I was not managing my tackle well; I lost bait after bait, and was so absorbed in gloom that Tony had to shout several times before I turned to see him with a curved rod, pulsing to the slow runs of a spring fish. This salmon stayed down with sullen power, at times yielding slowly, then running out another ten yards of line, in a way typical of the fight of early Slaney fish. Such struggles might last five or ten minutes, and for the duration one is focused on the line cutting this way and that through the water, and is aware only of a straining rod and a thumping heart.

After five minutes I netted a beautiful silver fish of eleven pounds; I was astonished. I had been prepared for a long day's toil, and on this, my first day proper of spring salmon fishing, we had one before lunch. We carried it over the ploughed field, stopped the traffic as we crossed the road, and mounted the steep hill to the hut where shelter and hot soup brought back the feeling to our grey faces.

After lunch we went to the lower half of the beat, with me leading. I had changed my end tackle and weights, and with the stimulus of Tony's catch I was fishing more purposefully. The three-inch Yellowbelly was making a smooth traverse of Doyle's Flat, a slick glide four or five feet deep, with crinkles of current rising from the weed fronds. The bait knocked the bottom every so often, and then came a double tap, sensibly different, so I was alert when the bait was seized and my first spring salmon pulled the rod into a taut curve. I cannot remember much of the fight, except seeing the salmon, holding steady three feet down in a strong flow, despite heavy pressure. It weighed seven pounds, and I have a photograph of it, a brilliant little fish reflecting sharp spring sunshine under a sky turned blue and white.

A bad day dulls the senses and you drive home a dismal introvert, unseeing and indifferent. That evening the austere spring fields and hedgerows, cleansed by winter floods and frosts to a distinctive March pallor, became part of my imagery of early spring salmon fishing.

We saw lots of fish that day, jumpers and splashers, and one arched out of the river at my feet in that brisk porpoise roll which is the sign of a running salmon. John Luce was then averaging a fish per day. On his first day a few seasons later, 28 February 1984, he took seven salmon, three between half past four and ten past five in the evening. It marked almost the end of the last really productive cycle on the river, and it was my good fortune to have had the small share in it which revealed to me the incomparable satisfactions of spring salmon fishing. This, more than any other angling I know, distils intense experience from rare events. To rods who expect a fish a day, a salmon landed is merely one's due. But when one fishes through a black easterly wind, spitting rain and hail, patiently covering the water foot by foot and sometimes doubting whether there is a fish within miles, and then one takes, it is a thing of wonder. It is almost worse when conditions are good, which happens only on rare days, and you still do not see, let alone meet, a fish. In spring salmon fishing, it is not the despair that gets you, but the hope.

There are also substantial pleasures in managing the big tackle required to fish a fly in early spring. I used to spin until the first of April, when fly only is the statutory rule on most of the Slaney, and I had great satisfaction from it. But increasingly I like to fish with a fifteen foot rod, a number eleven sinking line, and a tube fly. Sunk-line fishing is not practical on some beats and even where it may be practised, it can disadvantage many anglers. But a spring salmon is the greatest prize in angling, and it is the greater for having been taken through mastery of a difficult traditional craft.

*   *   *

The Slaney is a spring salmon river. The season begins in the early weeks of March and ends on the last day of August. The effective season lasts until the end of May, when the last run of spring fish, except in an unusually dry year, has come in. There are sea-trout from July in the lower river, and there is a substantial autumn run of late fish after the statutory closing date, but for all intents and purposes, salmon fishing on the river spans the months of spring.

The main salmon fishings begin below Aghade bridge, and end a few miles south of Ballycarney in county Wexford. The river rises in the Wicklow hills, in the Glen of Imaal, and runs into lowland country south of Baltinglass. Nowadays, largely because of modern drainage methods, run-off from agricultural land has been accelerated, and it behaves rather like a big spate river, rising and falling quickly. It is a fairly steep river, although much of its course is through lowland pastures. One unfortunate effect of the adjoining farmland is that spring ploughing leaves a lot of the land in tilth, and heavy rain washes this in. Nothing kills Slaney fishing so thoroughly as a big brown flood, and though water levels may drop to acceptable heights fairly quickly, the mud in suspension needs to fall out before the river returns to good fishing trim.

It is a river of medium size, and generally shallow; almost every springer I have had has come from water less than five feet deep. Most beats have good fly water; indeed the best beats are entirely composed of fly water in a succession of sharps and flats (the terms we Irish use for runs and glides). The strong flows of the early season require heavy tackle to fish a sunk fly effectively in cold water. But the river is an ideal medium for the small fly and floating line, and in late April and early May will fish throughout its length, given reasonable conditions. Then one can ply a floating line the whole day and expect a fish at any time. But as the days lengthen, and especially in hot or bright weather, late evening is the best time, and most experienced Slaney rods fish from about five o' clock into the gloaming.

*   *   *

The Slaney has never been comparable with the great salmon rivers in terms of numbers of fish. It produced returns in proportion to its medium size. In the good times this meant about a hundred fish a season from beats a mile long. There is a lot of reliable evidence for this. The doughty Mrs N. K. Robertson, whose *Thrifty Salmon Fishing* and *Further Thrifty Fishing* are largely about the Clonegall beat, gives figures of 100, 50 and 102 fish from about a mile of double bank in 1937, 1939 and 1941 respectively. The years 1945 and 1946 produced similar figures on the same length of water. T. C. Kingsmill-Moore provides supporting evidence in *A Man May Fish*: he had access to a mile of water which he fished only at weekends, and his best season in twenty-five years gave him thirty-seven fish, a good total even then for one rod on a spring river. Twice he had seven fish in a day, and several times five or six. He also caught a thirty pounder from it.

I fished part of this water, from the opposite bank, in the mid-1980s, and saw records of the length for the early 1950s. In the years 1950, 1951 and 1952 it yielded 73, 85, and 131 salmon.

The river fished well in the early 1960s but then was badly affected by UDN (Ulcerative Dermal Necrosis), and only recovered in the 1970s, when the latter years of the decade were particularly good, and on some beats returns equalled those of the early 1960s. A decline set in from the mid-1980s and became serious at the end of the decade. There were some signs of recovery in the mid-1990s, which were fostered by local and international initiatives. The graph of recent Slaney returns would roughly match those of many other spring fisheries in these islands.

The Slaney spring run starts early, and some fresh fish are usually about in February. But the main run occurs around April, and if I were to be restricted to one month on the river this would be it. On reasonable water the fish will be in and will have spread throughout the river, giving sport on all beats. Everyone fishes fly (under recent amendments from about the tenth of the month), at least between Aghade and Ballycarney bridges, and a fish may take in any hour of daylight. April fishing should improve considerably because under a local agreement the estuary nets do not now begin work until May; formerly they began in April. They had a decisive effect on stocks because the estuary, from Enniscorthy to the sea, is long and narrow, and the fish tend to linger in it until they sense it is time to move up. There was a 'slap' for forty-eight hours at the weekend, but this was never sufficient to provide a significant escapement of fish in the netting season.

*   *   *

The spirits of anglers past are at your shoulder on the banks of the Slaney. When I fished the Ganly water, just above Kilcarry bridge, I used sometimes to think of Kingsmill-Moore as I cast a line at the Ivy Rock, or the Fairy Seat, because he would have fished the stretch from the opposite bank. That lovely passage of water was good to me because I took a salmon from it the first time I fished it, on the evening of a raw March day in the 1980s. We had fished hard until then without sight of a fish, but the beat was new and full of interest so I carefully worked my bait, a buoyant Devon Minnow, around the weir at the Fairy Seat. As I moved downstream, I came to a high bank, with a narrow ledge below it, just above the water. I took my stance on this and let the bait fan through the shallowing tailwater of the weir. The fish took when I had reached the last casting position on the ledge, and must have been tired, because it neither ran far downstream, which would have finished me, nor very fast. I was able to tease it above me and play it in the currents of the weir. I hand tailed it out and killed it before heaving it up the eight foot bank and clambering after it. It shone in the evening light like found silver. This was, I think, the very run from which Kingsmill-Moore describes taking four fish, in very few casts, in *A Man May Fish*.

However, it is not so much Kingsmill-Moore I associate with this water nowadays as the late Bobby Ganly. Bobby with his brothers, David and Jim, fished all over Ireland. Jim's fishing book for the early 1950s sometimes records more than a hundred salmon to his rod alone in a season, taken from the Boyne, the Slaney, the Ridge Pool on the Moy, Ballynahinch, the Owenduff, Lough Conn and so on. Bobby was the one I knew best, and whether seated at the head of the table in Srahnamanragh Lodge on the Owenduff, or in the hut on his beat of the Slaney, he had a beguiling charm. I last met him on the Slaney, when the river was running very high and out of order, so we spent more time than usual in the hut, Bobby dispensing gin and tonics with a generous hand, and recounting his long experience of that water. He took us along the lower beat from the Sheeps' Rock, describing all the good lies. One of the unusual features of this water is that much of it has a shallow gradient, and weirs have had to be installed to accelerate the flow and create lies. Some of the best lies for salmon are on the very lip of these weirs, where a glossy bulge of water forms. Bobby got lots of his fish on flies eased across these places, and he pointed them all out to us that afternoon.

Slaney anglers often cross Kildavin bridge from the Carlow side, before turning for beats upstream or downstream. If you look left at this point you see

Opposite: A 12lb Slaney springer, March.

the river sweep around a turn before the Dereen enters, just above the bridge. This marked the lower limit of Mrs N. K. Robertson's water, described in the books I mentioned earlier. These are an invaluable source for the Slaney angler. They describe seasonal variations in the number of fish taken. They mark how temperature fluctuations, and water levels, affect the passage of fish over the course of the seasons. The relative number of salmon taken from the marked lies on the beat, for each of a number of seasons is also noted. The books are full of interesting data and acute observation, but narrated in a style all her own, which is arch, sometimes obscure, and endearingly snobbish.

Mrs Robertson lived in Huntington castle, at Clonegall, which subsequently went to her son Lawrence Durdin Robertson. He was for a time a vicar of the Church of Ireland, but had a revelation and became a priest of the cult of Isis. I do not imagine that the cult made great inroads into the Roman Catholic, or Church of Ireland, congregations of this part of Wexford. I once wrote to Durdin Robertson, enquiring if his water was let, and received a very courteous reply; at this time he styled himself Baron of Strathloch. Let no one think that Wexfords is a plain agrarian society.

Mrs Robertson mentions a character called the Goat, a gillie who accompanied one of her guest rods. There is some rather dubious colour in her description of him, which seems to have been the lot, in print, of Irish gillies of the day. Regardless of the accuracy of her description, I remembered it when I came upon his grandson on the riverside late one May day. John Donohue (known up and down the river as 'Silver') was himself a gillie, serving most of his time on the Wood beat. He is at least a third generation gillie, because not only his grandfather, but his father also, served in that honourable profession. We had an interesting chat, and then he set to work with his fifteen foot rod, a weapon of pedigree which had seen many a skirmish and showed evidence of perfunctory repair. Regardless of its looks he wielded it like a master, casting the whole of a sinking line, off either shoulder, from quite a difficult bank.

*   *   *

I have been able to fish almost all the beats on the Slaney, and although the river's overriding character is the excellence of the fly water from top to bottom, each beat is distinctive. Curiously the upper beats, above Kildavin, often have shallow gradients, requiring weirs and groynes to hold fish and push the water through more urgently. The lower beats, from the Wood, just above Bunclody, to Mountfin, all seem to have a quicker flow, which is not just attributable to the greater volume derived from tributaries.

Ballintemple is one of the first publicly accessible beats below Aghade bridge. The river is bounded closely through the whole beat by high banks, and on the upper part the river has itself cut deep so that one has to scramble down steep inclines to fish it. There has been much work done on this beat, by way of weirs and groynes, to improve lies. With high water it can fish well in the early season, but it really comes into its own from April, and in May this is one of the most beautiful beats, in its waters and its surroundings, on the whole river, offering superb floating line fishing. The Ganly water is immediately below Ballintemple, and continues to Kilcarry bridge. Soon after this the Huntington Castle water begins; then the Mount Leinster Anglers have about a mile of fishing.

The Wood water is the next stretch, and one of the finest beats on the river. It fishes well throughout the season, and in the early weeks is slightly less reliant on high water than beats above it. It is a steep beat, so travelling fish lie all along it. It is also one of the largest Slaney beats and one of the most difficult to get to know. There is no better place than the Wood for proving that the most knowledgeable and skilful salmon anglers will consistently do better than anyone else. You could put a competent angler on the Wood, in excellent conditions, and he might not touch a fish, but instead have Rory Harkin fish down it and he will come back with two or three. I have known him do it several times; even in the sulphurous heat of spring 1995 he had two fish from the beat in an evening in late May, when the flow was reduced to a trickle, and other rods had given up to sunbathe.

I will always associate the Wood with Cheltenham week of National Hunt racing. Many of the regular rods from this and other Slaney beats go off to lose their shirts in genteel Gloucestershire at this time, and in the past I have been an indirect beneficiary by getting a guest rod then, so my thanks are due to Joey O' Neill of Tullow. Some of the racing men are not beyond a little innocent mischief, and any advice, when you are at the bottom of a beat, about a certain fish at the top of the beat, should be scrutinised with care before you go for a mile-long hike through forest and bog, leaving your benefactor in sole possession of a good pool.

Bunclody is the main town on the salmon angler's Slaney, and really marks the divide between the upper and lower river. Clohamon weir lies just below Bunclody, and can form a barrier to running fish if either the temperatures are very low, or the water is low. This effect has been greatly reduced by an improved fish pass installed in the last few years. Below Clohamon is Mrs Kennedy Kish's water. This is one of the most productive beats on the river, and is particularly good in the early season. When the fish will not run through the pass they fall back, along the beat. Immediately below is the first of the Eustace fishery beats on the right bank, Moyeady. The left bank is still the property of the Skrine family, and the record Slaney fish is said to have been taken here by Major Skrine, in the run at the top of the beat called the Major's Stream. The Eustace fishery is unusual in that there are three beats, Moyeady, then Mountfin and the Glass Door, the latter two below Tombrick. Rods are rotated so that they fish one beat in the morning and the next in the afternoon. Immediately below this fishery, downstream of Ballycarney bridge, Jim Doyle and Ivan Shiel have a piece of water. Ivan is the doyen of Slaney anglers, and knows the river as well as anyone. The main fishings end a little downstream of here.

*   *   *

Although I got my first spring salmon from Tombrick, one of my most memorable fish came from Caulfields on the Wood which is one of the great pools on the river, and has been good to me, although I have always fished it as a guest of my friend Leslie Bryan.

35

Tony Cains landing an evening fish on the Slaney, May.

It was the 28 February, a bright but bitterly cold day. The narrow Wexford roads were treacherous and we set out late, hoping that the black ice lurking in the shadows of the tall hedgerows would have melted. It was approaching midday when we set up our gear. The river was full, but not carrying much colour. We would have said that it was in nice condition if we could have been sure that it was not rising. It was one of the worst ever beginnings to a season; this was the third day on the beat and no fish had yet been landed. There was little good news from elsewhere up and down the river, so our fishing was done carefully but not with great hope. We met a fisherman returning from the bottom of the beat, who had just fished through Caulfield's with no luck.

We used Devon Minnows, but semi-buoyant plastic ones, which when fished on a longish trace would float just above the rock and debris of the river-bed, tethered by the weight. For this early season spinning, the weight, and how it was used, was crucial. The essential thing was to judge the weight so that it would just ride the current, touching the rocks occasionally, but not so heavily as to lodge amongst them. If the judgement had been made correctly, the line, cast at forty-five degrees downstream, could be allowed to traverse the currents while the rod was held high. The Devon worked slow and deep, and its progress could be followed by the high line sagging from rod tip to water. The reel was not touched, unless the bait snagged, until the bait swung into the near side.

I fished down the first part of the pool, to the stream and the fence, and crossed over. The bait was working nicely, with the lead just touching bottom. Around the fifth cast beyond the fence, the bait was in the centre of the river when there was a soft knock, as if I had touched weed, and then a pull so powerful that it took the rod around and tore line from the multiplier. The fish continued into a fast run of more than fifteen yards before the pressure stopped it. For the next five minutes or so, it surged strongly up and down the pool, not showing itself until the end when, as it turned on its side, Leslie ran the tailer over it and then pulled it out like a cork from a bottle. It was a ten pound fish, and certainly the most beautiful of any species I have ever caught. Salmon fresh from the sea, in the cold waters of early spring, are incomparable for colour and line. This fish had a grey back, and on its flanks a faint lilac iridescence grading into pure silver. This was a midday fish, and that is one of the two most productive periods of the angling day in early spring on the river, the other being late evening.

The description 'spring salmon fishing' covers greatly variable conditions; take another fish which Caulfield's yielded me, on the first of May. I left at midday to fish the afternoon and evening. It was a close soft day, with just a little wind. Again there was good water, but this time I walked through thick grass, and the banks by sheltered pools like the Sallies were covered with primroses and a haze of bluebells.

I fished down with a fifteen-foot rod, a floating line, and a half inch aluminium tube attached to a slow-sinking leader. I reached Caulfield's without incident, and was fortunate to find no-one on the right bank. I have never had much faith in the broken water running into Caulfield's but this day I started there. Luckily, my rod was particularly well adapted for Spey casting, and I could cover the pool without worrying about any trees behind. The fish took on the far side, where the popply water settles as the river bed deepens. It all happened very slowly; the loop of line in my hand slithered out easily, I raised the rod, and a fish just under the surface, firmly attached. I played it for the regulation five minutes and then lifted out an eleven pounder.

Caulfield's looks a classic pool: there are rapids above and below, it is sheltered by trees, there is a good current and depth, and the salmon have the security of rocks under their bellies for the length of the pool. Lennon's pool on Moyeady is another great Slaney pool, although it does not shout it. In fact, superficially it is one of the least attractive pools on the beat. But it produces salmon and on my first morning fishing Moyeady, and the first time down Lennon's, I had my Devon taken by a very fresh eight-pounder. Lennon's is a flat, quite open except for a willow over the right bank at the very end, and it isn't deep. By rights, such a pool should fish best in the evening. But I have had fish from it, in midday, on the sunk line and big fly. Of course, the surface has to be broken to allow a chance, but on a day in mid-April a few years ago, the sky was quite bright, with passages of flock clouds, and a fairly gentle breeze blew. I had hoped for a fish upstream in the rough water of the Major's Stream, because I had seen some show, and there was good water. But I arrived at Lennon's blank, and my first casts, which seemed to crash down, did not reassure me. I persevered and the fly, a two inch black and yellow copper tube, was coming out of the main flow and I had started to handline, when the fish grabbed it on my second draw. It was a nine and three-quarter pound cock salmon, securely hooked in the scissors.

It takes confidence to fish these flats and shallow reaches with the deadly intent that makes a fly work properly. I am happy at Lennon's because I have had fish there. But the Upper and Lower Gravels on the Wood beat me completely and I fear I will never get a fish from them. The river comes down from Deacons, a lovely pool, sweeps around a broad corner and flows down, wide and clear so that one can see most of the gravel bed and the weeds for a couple of hundred yards. I have never raised a fish in it, although this is where experienced beat rods get salmon.

On the other hand some have little faith in Three Rocks, whereas friends of mine would fish nowhere else. I learned a thing or two about salmon behaviour here one May evening. Three Rocks is a fast run over a rubble of stones, about two hundred yards long. The right bank is a steep slope, heavily tree-lined so that the water beneath is almost permanently shaded, with exposed rock at the base against which the main run of current leans all the way down. It needs to be waded, because the line must be laid at an acute angle on this current to prevent the fly skittering. I have never been certain of which are the Three Rocks. There are big rocks in the river, breaking the flow, which might be them, but I have been told that they are in fact three rock buttresses, projecting slightly into the river on the right bank. On that evening I was guiding my fly around one of these , with the rod held fairly high, when I saw the sag of line rise, and gave way to the pull which took several feet of slack from my fingers. Then nothing. There was no question that this was anything but a fish, because I was using a small fly on a floating line; it had not touched an obstruction, nor had it been fouled by floating weed. I did not cast over the fish again immediately but

Playing a Slaney salmon hooked on floating line and small fly. The Wood Beat, May.

worked down to it slowly, and experienced a sequence of similar false takes, to flies of different sizes and weights. It was exasperating because fish in this lie are normally good ones. Tony took a twelve pounder from it, at about the same time of evening, a few weeks later.

*   *   *

The spring runs have been in decline everywhere for over a decade; the really big catches, of golden years like the early 1950s, are not even memories for most of us. But spring salmon fishing still exerts the most powerful magnetism. The fish, though scarce, are magnificent. Fishing a long line with a big fly rod is bracing, and there is the severe beauty of the early months, unfolding into glorious days in April and May when it is a joy to be on the riverbank. A. H. Chaytor said in his marvellous book, *Letters to a Salmon Fisher's Sons*, 'one good day's salmon fishing in spring is worth a week in late autumn, and I would not exchange one brilliant, glittering spring salmon for half-a-dozen autumn fish'. Spring fisherman on any water will immediately sympathise and feel again the longing to be abroad in that tonic air. When we Slaney fishermen meet to have a few drinks in the evenings, tired in limb, we round off some of the most satisfying fishing days of the angling year.

CHAPTER 4

The Mayfly

Opposite Robbie O' Grady's guest house in Ballinrobe is a cemetery, and behind it a stand of tall trees. On many a June morning in the 1980s, when I fished Mask every year at mayfly time, we used to step out to look at the trees, then in fresh green leaf, to judge the wind. The grey limestone of the cemetery walls and headstones, and the swaying green of the tall grasses and the trees, is an abiding memory of Ballinrobe. It is a town of old grey stone, fine eighteenth-century mill buildings, Georgian town houses, and double-stepped pavements on the steep streets. Many of the mill buildings are now unused, especially those around the River Robe which runs like a canal, within stone embankments, through the town. On the river, the locks are slowly disintegrating, and in June the foliage is thick and envelops the decaying masonry in soft greens. It is a beguiling place at dusk, when swarms of ephemerids rise from the limestone river, and innumerable small brown trout ring the surface as far as the eye can see.

Wind is probably the single most important influence in fly-fishing on the great limestone loughs of the west. Too little and the fish will not rise. Too much and it is dangerous to go afloat. So we always went out early to look at the trees, as they took their cue from the wind rolling off Mask just a mile or so to the west. Those mornings had ritual elements: a good cooked breakfast; the search for an engine in Robbie's bicycle workshop, involving the selection of a Seagull which was stood in a barrel of oily water, roughed up with spanner and sandpaper, and berated in the western tongue until it sputtered into life; getting the 'mixture' from a local garage, a matter of some moment as a stalled engine on the waves of Lough Mask is no joke; the collection of flasks and lunches. Then we drove to Cushlough, the main departure point on the eastern side of Mask.

In late May and early June, Cushlough was alive at this hour; boats rimmed the harbour, and anglers loaded gear and made up casts. Although Cushlough is sheltered, one can see the open lough just beyond the mouth of the bay, and the feel of the wind here, and the look of the wave, told you whether it was a good fishing day. The best day gave a warm southerly or south-westerly wind, at a steady ten or fifteen miles an hour, and low but well-defined cloud. One could count on fish rising to the mayfly in such weather.

The exit from Cushlough, and the routes through the lough, all have to be learned carefully. This is the most dangerous lough in Ireland, especially the eastern side, which, from the Rocky Shore in the north, southward past Cushlough to the mouth of the canal, is an archipelago of reefs and islets, beaten by waves which can have a fetch of five miles, and grow huge when driven by big winds. In these conditions no sane person goes out of the bay, but no matter, because it can give good sport; my friend Charles Benson had a four pound fish there on a dry Mayfly when the main lough was a maelstrom. The level of the lough fluctuates from year to year, and one cannot rely on seeing the rocks. There are always some – and they can be gigantic boulders or reefs – which lie just sub-surface, and can smash a boat, or at least give anxious moments if you run aground. I did this in my second year, luckily in a small wave, and two of us wrestled hard to slide the boat free.

We wouldn't have got on the water before ten o' clock but the late start mattered little, because the first mayfly rarely showed much before midday. We usually fished the grounds around Martins, Devinish, and Rialisk Islands, and the Black Rocks. The prevailing winds on Mask come from the direction of the Joyce mountains whose dark silhouettes recede into the distance on the south - western horizon. A favourite drift was from about a quarter of a mile south-west of the southern tip of Martins, with the boat guided on a course which took it on a diagonal just past that tip, into the bay, right up to the eastern shore. All of this was good ground, shallow and rocky. In promising conditions one would be on the alert as soon as turning the boat into the drift after having beaten upwind.

Any decent fishing wind on Mask soon unfurls a big wave, but the mayfly are surprisingly distinct, displaying an olive colouring against the grey water. Their wings catch the wind and make the fly list to one side, sometimes keeling them over. A Mask hatch is usually sparse, but even so the freshly hatched green fly often immediately bring fish up and on the take. So as soon as a mayfly was spotted, fish could be expected, and one looked for splashes in the waves, or small flat patches, both the most obvious signs of trout taking duns. Then the boat was trimmed to drift down towards the rises, the talking stopped and each angler was absorbed by a tense expectancy and fished with perfect concentration. The huge lough shrank at these times; you unconsciously absorbed the co-ordinates of the area where you saw the fish rise – aligning it ahead with the ruined house on the rise above the far shore, on the left with Martins, and on the right with a headland. You locked your eyes on that little area in the waste of rolling wave, and were not surprised when a swirl broke it and the raised rod bowed tight to a fish.

Mask fish need to be struck quickly, then they must be led around the back of the boat, where you play them with the rod hooped over the waves, the line taut and perpendicular, and wind and spray beating into your face. Often it happens that just at this point when every link to the fish is apparently secure, the rod springs straight. You lose a lot of wild brown trout on these loughs.

Fish take the wet-fly in many ways, some underwater, some splashing at the bob. I think that the best is when a trout shows, and dives out of the water to fall on the fly. Your heart stops because it is so sudden; but your hand does not get the message in time and keeps going, pulling the fly away. Then if you are quick and fire the fly in again, the fish, which will have been hunting around, will be on it in a flash. There was a fish at the Black Rocks that did this, and jumped at the fly just feet from me so that I could clearly see the spots on his arched body.

When I cast again the first draw met a solid thump and I was into a splendid trout, one of the silvery Mask trout, short and strong, which pulled deep all around the boat for several minutes before yielding, and yet weighed just over two pounds.

The whole craft of lough fishing is based on managing the drifts so that one is constantly covering productive ground. Trout take the artificial best in water between four and eight feet deep. As a rule of thumb, if an oar poked down vertically does not touch the bottom, the water is too deep for the artificial fly. Mask water is now a little more coloured than it was, but it was never clear; it was always stained with a faint colour, as if from peat. When you came upon a rock unexpectedly, it loomed suddenly as a great amber mass, rather than the natural limestone grey, due to the water acting as a colour filter. So one could not always see the deeper parts of the good drifts, and the boat might stray into dead water. This is where the services of a good boatman are invaluable, and on Mask there were none better than Robbie O' Grady or Jimmy Murphy of Cushlough. Robbie would guide the boat along the productive lines, following invisible underwater spines over which the trout were hunting unseen. A couple of anglers, both fishing, might control the drift by means of an oar trailing from the back of the boat and used as a rudder. However, the skill lay not just in boat handling, but in knowing the underwater terrain well.

The choice of drifts on Mask, even in the relatively restricted areas we fished, is bewildering, and they change with every point that the wind shifts. It is essential to keep searching for the fish, and not to repeat drifts over dead water. If we were out with Robbie we might try several lines of drift in the couple of hours between ten thirty and lunch.

We almost always had lunch on the sloping gravel of the east side of Martins island. The hump of the island, and the gnarled scrub oak and alder, sheltered us from the wind and let us light a fire in the embers dotted about the bank here, a resting place for decades for Mask anglers. We used an old volcano kettle, a brilliant design with a sleeve which holds the water, around a flue for the fire which heats the entire inner surface and boils the contents in no time. We used lough water then. It could be a lovely spot, and I remember lunches where I toasted under a warm sun in my waterproofs. However, a good fishing day was often a damp one, and there were also times when lunch, a wet sandwich, was taken by anglers soaked fore and aft.

The northern point of Martins slopes gradually underwater, into an inviting litter of boulders which often harbours a fish or two. I got one of my most memorable Mask fish here, when I elected to fish from the bank for a while, letting Robbie take my friends elsewhere. The margin was rough but fairly clear and allowed a backcast. I wandered along it until I came upon a cluster of trout taking mayflies – duns and nymphs – not far offshore. I tried a conventional nymph at first and got just knocks and nibbles. Then I put up a Wet Mayfly pattern, a classic wet-fly dressing for trout of the western loughs, and soon it was firmly taken by a good trout which led me along the bank before I could draw it to the net. It was a striking fish. In the water it seemed to have a pink flush on its flanks and, when landed, there were indeed great splotches of red and black on its sides, in a brilliant display of colour. This was a gillaroo, a fish of the

43

shallows which makes its living almost exclusively on molluscs, deriving its colouring from them. That two pounder was the first of a number of fish I took from this end of Martins, and convinced me that bank fishing for western lough trout is a serious proposition. I did it with profit in many other locations on Mask and also on Carra and Corrib.

The day would continue until four or five o' clock, and it was very important to fish with a will right to the end; although there was often a hiatus in mid-afternoon, and the hatch of mayfly would start to tail off, trout seemed to get a second wind as the fishermen tired, and we rose many over the years on the last drifts as we headed into Cushlough. Some of these would have been risen by a method which Robbie called side-casting, and were very difficult to hook. This is casting to the side from a boat moving at about half-speed, controlling the fly as it swings in a swift arc, and throwing it out again. Even at half-speed the boat is moving at a good clip, and the trout come at a dash to the fly. Usually one yanks it out of their mouths or just snicks them.

Back at Cushlough, at the end of the day, car boots which were carefully tidied before the trip became a jumble of damp waterproofs, tackle, nets and fish, tainted distinctively by petrol from the engine. We usually drove to Robbie's and left the cars there, while we walked to a pub in the town, for a brief post-mortem before a wash and dinner. One day I drove back to the house and found Robbie laying out fish on the grass beside the cemetery wall opposite. It was the best catch of wild lough trout I have ever seen or am likely to see; there were five, their weights roughly two, five, six, eight and nine pounds. All were taken trolling on that sunny day in early June.

The pub (there are a number of fishing pubs in the town) is a pleasant necessity for the mayfly angler in Ballinrobe, because intelligence on the day's fishing on Mask usually filters back there in the evening. So you may contentedly absorb your pint of stout, feeling slightly chilled and weather-beaten, and gradually find out the day's events on the lough. If you have not got the taking fly, or want to buy spares, you can get them in some of the bars. I got the best Wet Mayfly pattern I have ever used in the Abbey bar. It was a green pattern which looked gross when dry, but was very effective in a Mask wave.

*　　*　　*

The mayfly comes up on each of the western loughs at slightly different times. The earliest usually show on Carra, where fly are often up before the beginning of May and the hatch is thickest in mid-May. Corrib mayfly show at different times on this great lough which is over twenty miles long. On the northern lough, around the Dooras peninsula, the fly are usually up by the 13 May and local anglers who know this area well, like Paddy Kineavy of Dooras, arrange a week's holiday then. When that happens you may depend on it that one could hardly choose a better week. But sometimes the fly may be delayed for one or two weeks. The Corrib mayfly can finish abruptly, usually by the beginning of June, and the fish are then extremely hard to move to any fly for a while. The Mask mayfly season is just getting going at this time, and Robbie used to recommend the first or second weeks in June as the best. The Mask hatch is not as heavy as those on Carra, where I have seen the densest hatches of all the western loughs, or the Corrib, and goes straggling on to the end of June and beyond. Lough Conn's hatch is heaviest about late May, and it too can go on for longer than the usual fortnight. Lough Cullen, which adjoins Conn and has a good stock of free-rising smaller fish, also has good mayfly hatches, which are at their heaviest two weeks earlier, about mid-May.

Different traditions of fishing have grown up on each of the loughs. The longest established are probably those on the Corrib, where Oughterard has been associated with the mayfly season for more than a century. There is a gentility about Corrib fishing at Oughterard which gives it some of the character of a social 'season'. Dapping the natural fly is the method here. A friend of mine was once invited for a few days' fishing to a summer house on the Glan shore, just north of Oughterard. All the party, including the women, fished. There were

Mayfly fishing, Lough Mask.

several boats tied up at the private pier. Each morning the boatman would arrive to see that they were ship-shape for the day, and he would bale them out, release the oars, fit the engines and check the fuel. He would ensure that each one had a supply of freshly-hatched mayfly duns, called the green fly, housed in specially made ventilated boxes. At ten the party would go afloat and soon the boats would have settled into drifts, and each long rod would lay its length of floss on the breeze, dabbing the fly on the water, and fish easefully through the day. Somerville and Ross might have described it.

Dapping is the traditional method all over the Corrib. It is imperative to have fresh green fly because their bodies are tougher than flies which are on the point of transforming into spinners. The best dappers I know are the Kineavys of Dooras. I have mentioned that Paddy takes a weeks holiday then, as do his brothers. They fish the dap in all weathers, including in big waves and cold winds and take fish regardless. They also use the simplest of tackle, just a fifteen foot rod, a running line and a number ten hook, with two mayfly on it. Flies are gathered in the morning and at lunch. They can be picked off the undersides of leaves, and from the tall grasses on lee shores. They can also be got from drystone walls which ripple over the bigger islands like Illaunribbeen. You have to look for the fly to find them, because they hide in the interstices of the stones, but once you spot one you see tens and a good crop can be picked in no time. The fly is laid on the water in front of the boat, let rest, picked off and laid down again, and so on. Fish take very close. The most important attributes of this fishing are sight and concentration, both of which are difficult when the lough is rough, and although it is May your feet are numbed from cold. The dapped natural produces wonderful catches; the most interesting that I have seen was a brown trout of three pounds, and a salmon of over thirteen pounds, taken by an angler in a few hours fishing one evening from the South Lake (the southern part of the lough) off Dooras. Salmon run through the Corrib along the western shore and anglers from Dooras occasionally take them during the mayfly season.

*   *   *

The wet-fly is also fished on the Corrib but does not have the primacy it does on Mask, where especially on the eastern side it is quite unusual to see the dap. It is the main method on loughs Conn and Cullin. Wet-fly involves standard lough tackle, and the use of a range of specialised flies. The Wet Mayfly, a generic name for a range of patterns all tied in roughly the same style, is one of the great western flies at this season.

My favourite Wet Mayfly is made like this: take some pheasant tail fibres, a cream badger cock cape and an olive cock cape, both a little soft, cream synthetic yarn, mallard flank or breast feathers dyed pale green and yellow, gold wire and primrose tying thread. This is the tying I know; there are variants, some involving French partridge feathers, but these are expensive and the humble mallard feather does the job just as well. Wind the thread in touching turns to the bend of a stout number ten or eight hook, (a Partridge G3A for choice). There, tie in three pheasant tail fibres by their butts, splaying out the tips behind the bend by tensing the thread. Then secure the wire, a badger hackle, and the yarn in that order, and bring the thread forward to the shoulder. Now wind on the yarn loosely so that it fluffs up, and tie in; bring the badger hackle forward over it, and after that the wire, in an opposing spiral, bedding it into the turns of hackle stem. Cut the ends neatly, because you need plenty of room at the head of this fly. Now for the hackles: tie in the olive cock first, and choose one that is long in the flue. Use all of it. Then tie in the mallard, a yellow or green, by the tip, which has been trimmed to give the thread a purchase. The fibres need to be persuaded to flare as you wind. Secure the head and trim the waste. The complete fly has a wide skirt of hackle trailing beyond the hook bend, and the relatively soft mallard is buttressed by the olive cock, and the palmered badger.

I have had some great fishing with the yellow hackled version of this fly on the Long Shallow off Oughterard on the Corrib. This is a reef, perhaps half a mile long, way out in the lough. You fish shallowing water as you approach it, and then you can usually cross it, if the water is not too low, with a few bumps and scrapes, and fish the deepening water on the far side. Fish take well immediately either side, sometimes rushing from the cover of boulders in very thin water. My wife and I had eight fish in a couple of hours here one day, many of them beautifully-coloured yellow trout; hers were to a dapped artificial fly. The fly in a fish's mouth looked quite a modest thing, but I was appalled at the volume of its hackles when I first saw this dressing. The long mallard fibres, and the secondary and body hackles, completely masked the hook, yet there is reason in it, because it is a dressing for big rough waters, where mayfly hatch out in two or three foot waves. You need a bushy fly with lots of hackle to work in these conditions.

I usually fish only two wet-flies, a Wet Mayfly on the top dropper and a slimmer dressing, perhaps an Invicta, on the point. Many anglers fish three, but they can be troublesome in a really big wind, when tangles can become impossible to unpick. A six pound test leader is sensible, because fish take the bobbed fly with a wallop, and eight pound material is better when it is very windy.

*   *   *

Wet-fly fishing on big water is a rugged sport which matches the wilderness of the western loughs. Spent gnat (mayfly spinner) fishing couldn't be more different. It is angling which demands quiet, precision, and discrimination. In a day's mayfly fishing with wet-fly you might cast over five hundred times; in an evening's spent gnat fishing ten could be enough.

There is generally little Spent Gnat fishing done on the big loughs. There was wonderful fishing on Lough Derg, the biggest lough on the Shannon system, in the middle years of this century. The best of it was at Whitegate and Mountshannon, and Tom Perry wrote about it in one of the interesting Irish small press fishing books (*May madness! Fifty years of fishing on Shannon, its tributaries, and amusing incidents*. Belmont (Offaly) Thomas G. Perry [1984]). Derg mayfly fishing was and is almost exclusively spent gnat fishing. The hatches of green fly are massive and the biggest I have seen anywhere except on Sheelin, but the fish are not interested in them. They really want the spent fly. Although

47

Landing a trout taken on a Wet Mayfly, Lough Carra.

the glory days of Derg fishing are long past, some enormous trout are still taken at Mountshannon, as they are upstream at Lough Ree. Derg fish are very handsome. The best I got was three pounds, while fishing a Wet Mayfly at Mountshannon, and it was a short, solid, very silvery fish, one of the hardest fighting trout I have hooked anywhere.

Nowadays the best Spent Gnat fishing is on loughs like Arrow and Carra in the west and Lough Sheelin in the midlands. For good Spent Gnat fishing there needs to be a lot of green fly, and all these loughs have heavy hatches. A really

48

Lough Derg trout taken on Spent Gnat.

big hatch on a lough is an extraordinary sight. I have seen the surface of Carra apparently covered by mayfly at a density of about one every two square yards for as far as the eye could see. The hatches on Derg, although more localised, were even heavier. But the biggest hatches were those on Sheelin in recent years, when at midday fly came off in huge numbers and covered trees and grasses on islands and the lee shores.

The fly pick a quiet site, metamorphose into the final adult stage, mate and then the females head for the water to lay their eggs. The mating swarms on Sheelin are dense columns, stacked way above tree tops. They head for the water as the wind drops, and lay exhausted when the eggs have been deposited. The numbers are incalculable; I have seen densities of more than one per square foot, with fly still falling like flakes of soot. This is when the fish move to them, and why Spent Gnat fishing is largely evening sport. But it is not exclusively so, and the morning after a heavy spinner fall, in calm conditions, the trout will

49

continue to mop them up in quiet corners where the corpses are massed by surface drift. These are often big fish, difficult to get near. Also, towards the end of the mayfly season, spent gnat can fall during the day, and give really good fishing then. Read Tom Perry's description, on page 93 of his book, of such a day on Lough Ree, when he and his wife took seven trout between three pounds and almost seven pounds, for a total weight of thirty-five pounds: but also note that this was a very exceptional day in every respect.

Spent Gnat fishing is target fishing for individual trout. It is high risk fishing in that conditions must be just right. The wind must be light; if it blows too heavily the mayfly will not be able to fly out against it. The air should be warm, and the water should be fairly calm, or rising fish are difficult to see. Even then the fishing can be difficult, because in a perfect calm trout cruise around unpredictably, and it is hard to anticipate them. We have sat through evenings on Sheelin with fly on the water, a smooth surface, and trout up and moving, but none within range, so that we cast less than a dozen times all told. Good fishing can be had on evenings with light breezes, providing the fly can get out. Then, in a general ripple, calm lanes will concentrate both fly and fish, which will tend to move upwind, and the artificial can be placed confidently in front of them.

This fishing is best done with an angler and a boatman because there are two separate jobs. One is to find the fish and to keep the boat within casting distance, but not to drift over them. The other is to get the fly to the fish, which requires concentration and accurate shooting. I have done it with a friend, when we fished turn and turn about, so that each of us took to the oars at agreed intervals, but even this can be a strain when there are very big trout about.

On Arrow and Carra, anglers sometimes fish from the islands, because the fly drop after a short flight and the fish come in close. This, when circumstances allow, is ideal. At other times, the boats lie in tight to the islands with shipped oars and wait for trout to show, then go out after them.

This is the main tactic on Sheelin, a lowland lough lying among green hills, less dramatic in scale and surroundings than the western loughs. Its waters are enriched by a limestone base, and have been recovering their clarity after years of contamination from agricultural pollution.

You pick up your boat at five or six pm, perhaps on the Upper Inny, then move down the narrow little limestone river, scattering small trout before you, out into the lough, and turn west along the sandy shallows, past Curry's Point and on to Church Island. A lot of the big Sheelin trout, wild fish from six to ten pounds, caught since the return of the mayfly, have been taken in this area. Other boats will be there, pulled ashore or lying in the lee of the island. Until the fish show, the boats lie side by side, their anglers sharing cups of tea and conversation, and casually watching for a sign that the business of the evening is about to begin.

More will come out, and on some evenings they may be uncomfortably numerous. Some may be new to the fishing and let impatience get the better of discretion; they motor under full power, and clatter oars. Spent gnat fishing in the old days had certain protocols which were generally enforced. The import of these was to give other boats plenty of sea room, and not to disturb the water, especially by indiscriminate use of the engine. When Tom Perry was learning the ways of spent gnat fishing on Lough Derg, from a local expert, Major Gibson, he was taught to cut the engine when five hundred yards from a likely spot.

Your tackle for delivering the spent artificial should have an emphasis on speed and accuracy, so it will be quite different from the gear needed for wet-fly fishing. A nine foot rod with a crisp action, capable of firing a WF7F line quickly, is needed. The artificials are quite big so a leader of about seven pound test is mandatory. A wide range of spent patterns is used, among them the Grey Wulff. I like a simple black and white fly, with tails of pheasant tail fibre, a white or cream synthetic floss body, wrapped with a bold black floss, and a soft black cock hackle, either tied full, or half circle (like the Mosely May), with the fibres of the lower half wrapped up horizontally, so that none protrude on the lower side of the hook. It is as well to have a wet-fly outfit made up too, because if the water does not allow spotting and tracking of individual fish, the only other option is to fish wet and hope to rise one of the big fish which are about in the late evening.

As the light dims, and the fly begin to fall, it is time to look out for trout. In a calm it is as well to lie in to the shore or island, and get a long view of the water in front. The fly will be falling more thickly close to shore, and this is often where the first fish show. When one is spotted, its course needs to be assessed before the boat is moved into position and the attack is made. Very often it goes down, or its course is erratic, and the opportunity to cast never comes. Even if the fly can be put down, it needs to be very close, because even in the early stages of the fall there are an awful lot of flies on the water. This can go on for the entire evening, and be very frustrating.

There is a little more chance for taking the initiative when a light breeze stirs the water. The boat can be positioned near calm lanes, at the windward end if possible, and in the rippled water, so that the oars do not disturb them. The flies will be more concentrated and so will the fish and, just as important, their movement will be more predictable.

It is possible to spend several evenings at this and not hook a fish. And in some years, because of cold or wind, the entire spent gnat season can be poor. In the season just past, more big fish were got on Sheelin on the Murrough, a large red sedge, fished in late June and July, after the mayfly, than on the Spent Gnat.

But no matter that the fishing is frustrating and that in truth the chances of coming across a big one are slim: this is great angling. Sight fishing for big wild trout – and fish over ten pounds are up in the surface – on a lovely lough, with a dry-fly, is unique. It is a tradition on the midland loughs as old as dry-fly on the chalk streams, and still an authentic experience. Long may it continue.

Following page: Fishing Bog Bay, Oughterard, Lough Corrib.

CHAPTER 5

Lodge Fishing

There is a romance about sporting lodges in wild places that found memorable expression in W.H. Maxwell's *Wild Sports of the West*. Maxwell's tale was ostensibly fiction, the story of a dashing military man who stayed, at the invitation of a noble cousin, in his shooting box in the wastes of north Mayo. Actually, it was based on his own picaresque life as a sporting clergyman, far more sporting than clerical, and his adventures when staying at Croy Lodge, as a guest of the Marquis of Sligo. Maxwell was a visitor there from 1819 until the 1830s (he had rooms in the garrison at Castlebar), and his book was published in 1832. Anyone who loves the west and its sport should know this book, which gives one of the earliest and liveliest descriptions of it. It is all the better for being a sympathetic view which respects the spirit of the place and its people, unlike much of the bad writing which followed it.

To every Irishman the west is a space of wilderness and freedom. This is partly a myth (Maxwell's book is one of its earliest invocations), but we live by such myths; so the west has long been a region of the Irish mind, where history and legend are mingled. Of all the west, few places are as wild as north Mayo; from Achill to Erris Head, the indented rocky coastline gives way inland to blanket bogs and the foothills of the Nephin Beg range, with each distant farmstead measuring out its own isolation. But when Maxwell was here in the 1820s, this was, in his own words, the *ultima thule*, the most far-away, unknown part of civilised Europe. The roads were mere tracks, opened to wheeled traffic only by the outdoor relief schemes of the famine decades. They were sometimes so bad that people of the region had to bring their grain to market by means of ships, which skirted a treacherous coast, and Croy Lodge itself had to be provisioned from the sea. Men made a living out of selling otter pelts, and there were still eagles on the cliffs of Achill Island. There were also great numbers of game birds, especially grouse, on the moors, and salmon in the Owenduff, on whose estuary Croy Lodge was built. Maxwell is often an unreliable witness, but he gives the authentic flavour of a rough vigorous sport, describing nights spent in a small hut on the high moor when his party were shooting grouse; or late evening celebrations in Croy Lodge, when, befuddled by a close cabin atmosphere, compounded of peat smoke and whiskey fumes, he would take the midnight air by the river nearby, to clear his head.

Francis Francis, the Victorian angling writer, fished the Owenduff and the neighbouring Owenmore in the mid-nineteenth century. He describes the original character of the flies used there in pages 378 – 381 of *A Book on Angling*

53

(second edition, 1867), quoting a letter from a friend, S, who rented the Owenduff for several years: 'The flies of the Owenmore and Owenduff rivers some years ago were always what is called "jointed", and were made in two ways; the first had the joints made of hackles of divers colours, tied in as a pattern I send you . . . The enclosed is a specimen from the Dee, in Aberdeenshire, to which river it was transported by Mr. Gordon, from Ballycroy, and has since been naturalised'. Francis adds in a footnote: 'I never could understand how the Nicholson, which was a regular Erris notion, got on to the Tay, but the course of its introduction seems pretty clear from the above. The fly referred to strongly resembles the Nicholson'. It is remarkable that this relatively small river, even now little known, but in the nineteenth century extremely remote, should have had an influence on such grand rivers as the Dee and the Tay. A little later in the letter S mentions killing 48 salmon and 137 white trout in a week on the Owenduff. According to Francis white trout in the Owenduff then ran up to six or seven pounds, and averaged two to three pounds

Croy Lodge has not changed much, although it is no longer a sporting lodge; it is on private land and cannot be approached without permission. As you look past the gable end you still see the ocean waves running into the estuary of the Owenduff, just as Maxwell described, and farther westward the grey loom of Slievemore on Achill Island, vaporous in Atlantic mists.

*   *   *

Almost all the fishing on the Owenduff is divided between lodges, many of them old, roomy, slightly shabby and supremely comfortable after a day on the rough turf. It is good to come back, wet and muddied, and to win the race for a big cast-iron bathful of hot amber water; then to nurse your glass before the peat fire, seated in a crackled leather chair, waiting for the summons to dinner.

The great advantage of our lodge is that we are looked after by Theresa. At her call we go to the dining room, where the long mahogany table holds a succulent joint and the only crisp vegetables for miles. The way we work is that each rod brings the makings of one good breakfast, and dinner, with wines, and we all chip in during the week for any necessary extras. Theresa then converts this into memorable meals. Before I ever went to the Owenduff, I was chatting to a fellow angler one evening in Oughterard, and he told me about a week on a river in the west – a week remembered entirely in terms of food. He had been staying at our lodge. I only understood when I actually went there. Although we can see the river through the big dining room window, dinner is an interlude of ease and some of my most contented hours during these weeks have been spent at the table. We are a sober bunch so we do not hit the poteen, or attack the entire week's stock of drink on the first night. Maxwell would have found us very staid; his great objection to Sir Humphrey Davy's *Salmonia* was its suggestion that one bottle of claret constituted an evening's entertainment for four stout men. Assembling a fishing party is skilled work, and the individuals must be carefully selected to produce a happy crew like ours; Maxwell would have been a bit rich for our blood, but I know plenty of weeks on the river when he would find company much to his liking. The talk goes on over cheese and coffee and then at about eight o' clock we either go out for an hour upriver, or set up tackle for twilight fishing in the estuary.

There is a sense of privilege in the enjoyment of this, although in monetary terms the outlay per head for most lodges is less than for a package holiday in the sun. History has something to do with it. Until quite recently, these waters were privately owned, and accommodation and fishing were available only to guests of the proprietors. It is also partly because in experiencing the pleasures of a western moorland spate river, one is enjoying a very traditional form of sport. This is not big money tourist angling where ten or twenty fish days are the selling point. Each of the Owenduff lodges might average fifty to a hundred salmon or grilse in a season. A party of four rods would have enjoyed a very good week if they had got between five and ten salmon or grilse and some sea-trout.

The Owenduff has a run of early springers but it has fluctuated greatly in recent times. For example, in April 1993, a party of three rods had a good week taking six prime springers. The following year the spring take was poor, despite the fact that neighbouring rivers, especially the Moy, saw a strong revival of the spring run, Then a couple of years on, one rod had ten springers for his April week, with other rods in the party adding a further six. Things are complicated by the fact that some lodges may get fish, while others find their water barren.

Usually the first big run of Owenduff fish comes in late May or early June. These may be late spring fish or grilse. I have seen a catch of Owenduff fish averaging nine pounds taken at this time of year. After the main grilse run has come in, in late June or July, small runs may follow on spates. July and August see the main run of sea-trout arrive. The Owenduff has an excellent run of sea-trout, which was sustained while other west coast fisheries in recent years were blighted, and the river is worth fishing in August for the sea-trout alone. They take well during high or falling water, and run up to two or three pounds. The average weight here is quite high.

Some of the smaller local rivers had runs of very big sea-trout, and the Ballyveeney was the most notable for these. It is a narrow but deep river, which runs into the sea near Achill. In its prime it regularly produced sea-trout over six pounds, but latterly the runs have stopped.

* * *

When I knew no better, I thought that a spate river was a spate river, but in the west there are several different types of spate river. The Sheen river in county Kerry falls in cascades from pool to pool, each cupped in a basin of rock. The Erriff in Mayo flows in gravelly runs and big slow pools, between rough pasture lands in a narrow, dramatic valley.

The Owenduff meanders through high moors, and is approached over quaking bog for much of its course. A week's fishing here has many sources of satisfaction. There is the sense of well-being from vigorous walks over rough ground; the beats are long – perhaps three or more miles of tussocky peat banks, which soon gives tone to flabby muscle. There is a greater sense of isolation here than in any other Irish fishery I know. The beat I fish has a small farm at the top, and the next habitation one sees in many tens of square miles is two and a half miles downstream. When there is water, the river flows with an urgent push for almost its whole length, so that there is continuous fishing.

Fishing a spate river is always chancy, so a week is bound to come when you arrive in the middle of a heatwave, with no prospect of water for the duration of your stay. You must accept it like a good sportsman. Furthermore, when you leave the following Saturday, as heavy rain begins to fall, you must wish the best of luck to the asterisked entity who is head of the syndicate just taking over for the week, and congratulate him on his good fortune. This is always our way, though I quickly add that we hand over to very nice people who deserve their sport.

The dry river is a pathetic sight that saps the morale of an angler at a glance. Apart from the deep pools, the runs are shallow, and even a fine stretch like the Junction Pool is shrivelled and every stone in its bed revealed. Upstream the river is thin, choked with blanket weed, and showing barren sand. Some pools are still deep enough to hold fish – the likes of the Red Bank and Maudies – and if there has been a recent fresh, and the day is cloudy with an upstream wind

Good water on the Owenduff.

putting a wave on them, there will be a chance of a salmon. But it is usually an outside chance, and one has to wait for water to put a life-giving current into the stale channels again; then, beginning from the top of a beat, one can work down the whole length, and hook a fish anywhere. The country is broad moor as far as the eye can see, and the river flows in a classic sequence of pool and run.

As on most spate rivers, one can, and should, travel very light; long walks over bog and rock invigorate the body and relax the mind, but are not easy in good, wet, spate fishing weather. There will be side streams to wade, and miry ground and peat hags to hopscotch across; a fishing bag or suchlike become hateful bits of impedimenta when the going is soft. A rod and landing net, and a sandwich in your pocket, are quite enough. On this river, which is narrow and where wading is unnecessary, a single-handed rod, nine to ten feet long carrying a number seven line, is adequate for all seasons and water heights except perhaps big water in spring when a double-hander may be useful. Basic tackle selection is fairly straightforward. Far more important is a knowledge of lies, and minor tactics, which can make all the difference on a spate river.

Of lies, all that can be said is that they must be learned, from a gillie or an experienced rod, or from native wit and hard graft. A useful tip on lies is that if one is located, it is usually best addressed from a particular bank. If an approach on one bank fails, it's worth crossing over and trying a different line of attack, even though the river is narrow and a moderate cast from either side will seem to cover it all. One August day I fished a nice pool below a little bridge from the left bank. The current was diverted by the bridge arches into a strong run under the right bank, and then fanned out as it spread down the pool. I fished it all without stirring a fin. When I crossed over I immediately took a nice sea-trout of two pounds from mid-pool, where the crease line of the flow met a back eddy. The next cast travelled only a couple of feet, when a grilse pulled the rod over and then ran all over the pool. I must have covered both fish minutes before, but the swing of the fly from the right bank did the trick.

I lost that fish after a couple of minutes, because I was not sufficiently careful. A strong wind was blowing driving rain into my face, and the salmon, having ran downstream, then came back up deep under the far bank, and made as if to run up under one of the bridge arches. I turned it by hard side strain, but swung it over to my side of the stream, directly above me. I was walking it down when it suddenly ran into a cavity under the bank and transferred the hook. Salmon and grilse on small rivers often do this, and when you can anticipate them they can be turned out into the stream, provided your rod is not too short. I suspect that the behaviour is related to the relative lack of shelter in shallow spate streams with plain river beds. One often sees grilse and salmon rolling or turning, right in among the cover provided by marginal weeds, and they seem to seek similar shelter when hooked. Owenduff fish fight hard: the toughest salmon I have ever hooked, which took twenty minutes to land, was from Fletcher's Pool; it was a ten pound fish, one which I would normally expect to bank in five minutes, but this cock fish circled deeply with unyielding stamina and was not totally spent when I netted it.

The tidal fishing in the Owenduff estuary can also be good – on the flood tide for sea-trout and in high water for salmon. The sea-trout, which generally tend to be small, seem to be permanently present in the estuary in large numbers, and I have never fished for any length of time, at any point along its length, without at least hooking one. The best time for them is at dusk, especially when this coincides with high tide, but you can also enjoy midge-free fishing during the day and get fish, though not so many.

We use old tackle for this work, because the water on a flood tide is very brackish, and the salt content corrodes reels and flies, no matter how carefully they are washed afterwards. The banks of the estuary are rough, with slippery rock and deep pools, and care is needed in the dark. It is good fishing on a calm night or one with a slight ripple. The splashes of the advance guard of sea-trout shoals can be heard far off. There is often a heavy crash as a salmon jumps, offering only a false promise as we have never hooked a salmon here in the dusk. But we have had lots of sea-trout, and as the swirls approach you know that your lure will soon be hit. The fly needs to be about a size eight or ten, with a silvery dressing, and retrieved fairly fast. It will be nudged and nibbled before a fish grabs it in earnest and then dashes about in the shallow water, throwing ripples into the lighted patches. The fishing comes alive in phases; the fish run up past your position and you have takes every cast, then the splashes move up with the tide and the river in front of you is empty. Another wave of fish moves in and past and your rod is busy for another while. We have never spent more than a couple of hours at this, so it is not serious night fishing for sea-trout, but rather a diversion with sporting little herling. Some of us fish a worm off the weir (all methods are allowed in estuary waters) and get the odd sea-trout, but more often the small eels that wormers so richly deserve. It puts everyone in particularly good humour to watch a big angler, his wits slightly clouded by drink, try to unhook a very small eel in the gathering dusk.

The salmon, as far as I know, are only caught when a lot of floodwater is coming down. Then, when the main river is unfishable you may get a fish in the estuary; but you have to know just where to fish, because even here, the salmon are particular.

*   *   *

When conditions are right on your home water you will hardly go elsewhere. You know it well, and a salmon angler's greatest capital is not tackle or suchlike trivia, but his knowledge of the water, built up carefully over many visits. It is slowly accumulated, and qualified by experience. Each week on the beat adds to the store, and many of us will have spent several years getting to know one water. In favourable conditions, that knowledge can be put to good use. But when the sun shines and the river is warm, then you have the freedom not to fish, but to walk the high moors, or swim in the sea, or sit with a good book by the home pool, hearing the stale fish jump there.

If only the river is out of sorts, then it is a boon to have other fishing nearby, and the Owenduff is very well placed in this regard. We often have a day on lough Carrowmore, just ten miles up the road. Our week in late May is also quite a good time on the Moy, and it is not too far to travel for the chance of a late spring fish, if they are there. And although the lough Conn mayfly will not yet be up, those on Cullen will, and a day on that lough with its small but free-rising browns is far better than toiling on a sullen river.

*   *   *

The joy of lodge fishing is in its freedom. One can fish all day, or for an hour, and whenever one likes. I am an early riser, and I have always loved to be out on the river or lough in the grey hours, before the gentleman angler is abroad. Some years ago we had a lodge holiday in Kerry which was ideal for early fishing. As soon as light began to seep through the thin curtains over the french windows, I would listen for the sound of rain, or the low roar of a big flood coming down. We had a lot of weather that week, and one or two mornings a heavy brown spate rolled off the mountains, and I stayed in bed. But usually, when I padded over the bare boards to the window and looked out, I saw reasonably good water in the river, running just ten yards away. I used to leave stealthily, passing sleeping wife and children, and a sleeping angling companion who prefers gentleman's hours. The lodge was a noisy building – door catches rattled and floorboards creaked – but I always got to the hall without rousing anyone. There I took my rod off the rack, opened the front door, and I was on the river. It flowed right down to the lodge, and met there a big retaining wall which diverted it at right angles, eastwards, under a suspension bridge.

Dawn in Kerry is like dawn anywhere else in these islands, cool and damp. Its aesthetic appeal has been celebrated by people who must have experienced it from their beds. Animal life is astir in the early hours and I have always felt that it gives the chance to trick big old fish when their guard is down.

I used to fish the Planks first, some fifty yards upstream, and then perhaps the run above it, by the GAA football pitch. After that, I went back down river to make a wobbly journey over the suspension bridge. From here there were a number of nice runs stretching about half a mile in all, down along the left bank.

After a couple of hours I would have fished, briskly, through the main pools. I never came back with a salmon; I did not even rise one. But I had the river to myself, and for a while I was a free, alone, living on my nerve ends as the fly worked runs and glides in the concentrated stillness of the early day. A few people disapprove of early or late fishing as something which smacks of fishmongering and unfair play. But when I have to go out at a fixed time, and to be back for tea, it will be for a round of golf. The urge to fish is an instinct for the wild and you are near the source at five o' clock in the morning. I would return to the quiet of the lodge to grill rashers of bacon and sausages, make toast and coffee, and rouse wife, children, and sleeping gentleman angler for their breakfast.

Although I did not get a salmon on any of my early mornings, I did have some sport with sea-trout. However, on our second day, Leslie, the gentleman angler, made his way to the river at ten o' clock, like a leisurely boulevardier, shaved, breakfasted, and tweeded, and had hardly wet his fly when a grilse took it. I had fished the same run at six o' clock, when the water looked ideal and the world was quiet – and the grilse was asleep.

I was in a fortunate situation. The fishing on spate rivers usually has to be booked in advance, and so we all take pot luck. In addition, there may be beat rotation and some restrictions as to when one may fish. The rules are rational in these days of high demand; but the ideal arrangement for spate river fishing is to be beside the water, and to have complete freedom as to when to fish. In low water, or with stale fish, early or late can offer the only chance of a take, particularly with fly-only fisheries. Coincidentally, this is the arrangement which best suits those of us with non-fishing spouses and small children to amuse on a family holiday, and this kind of spate river fishing is a case where a family holiday and angling can be harmoniously accommodated in the one week.

I was on the Sneem river in county Kerry, one of the few spate rivers in Ireland to offer this degree of freedom, and one which really suits the family angler. My early morning forays gave me a couple of hours fishing, and I did not fret about what I was missing when later we took the children to the beach. The river and the fishing lodge formed a single let; unusually, this was the whole river, about five miles long from a lough in the hills to where it enters the sea, half a mile below the lodge (called the Huts), in the pretty little village of

Sneem. The lodge was on the edge of the village, just a few hundred yards' walk away. It offered standard fishing/shooting lodge accommodation – worn but comfortable amenities for bodies weary from exertions on the river bank or peat bog, plus plenty of hot water, turf fires, and warm beds. In the evenings I often used to settle down with a cup of tea and one of the fishing logs, going back to the 1940s, which had fulsome entries for the good days, and weary complaints about netting and poaching in the bad times. Around me was the flotsam of a sporting lodge: several packs of cards, not one of them a full set; burned down candles, old runs of the *National Geographic*; Agatha Christies and Alastair Macleans and more; beaten carpets and battered chairs. In other words, everything required to fold a snug sense of comfort around the holiday fisherman.

Spate river sea-trout.

The lodge was built a few yards from the river, at a right-angle bend, where the deepest pool, Pol na Leige, is found. It almost always holds resident salmon, whose jumps or rolls can be seen and heard from the sitting room, and by the end of a blank week they can provoke sinful thoughts, featuring naked pink baits, on this fly-only water. You can look out at any time and see if it is a fishing day or a beach day, because beyond the river a headwater stream cascading down the distant hills is an excellent indicator of a coming flood. Usually there is a barely perceptible ribbon; in heavy rain this may spread into two streams, or in really heavy water into one wide stripe on the mountainside.

If it was not a fishing day on the home water, there were good alternatives. Another attractive spate river, the Sheen river, was to be found about twenty miles east at Kenmare. This is a river of quite a different character, very steep and flowing in narrow gushing streams between pools cupped in rock. Fishing can sometimes be arranged through the Sheen Falls Hotel. Lough Currane was about twenty miles west, just beyond Waterville.

The Sneem is a lowland spate river. The upper course, including the parent lough, is rarely fished except for small brownies. This may change when a proper fish pass is installed in the lough outflow. The lodge rods usually only fish the lower portion of the fishery nowadays, that is to say below Pluais na gCat (the refuge of the pine marten), where the river is crossed by a road bridge. In the past, as the fishing book attests, fish were taken much higher up the river than they are now. But even then, pools which produced most fish were those downstream of where the Ardsheellhane flows in, a couple of miles above the lodge.

The first of these is the Run, a classic stream where the river is pinched in and the current is diverted against the far bank. It has rocks at the head, an eddy behind them, and a liveliness which is promising even in low water. I saw my first Sneem grilse caught here. The next good pool downstream is the Planks, where planking on the near side allows one to walk under a high bank and address fish lying in a stream which glides over a slowly shelving riverbed as it falls into Pol na Leige. A little below, fish also lie about the rocks under the swing bridge, but this is primarily sea-trout water, and I have had good sport in the early morning with fish which shot up out of deep water to take the flies here. The runs around the island downstream can be good in heavy water, and big salmon were caught under the left bank, beneath overhanging trees, in the past. This length is best fished from the right bank.

The Bathing Pool is another holding pool, good for sea-trout or grilse, but best early or late because it is flat water. The prime holding areas are groups of rocks (usually hidden in high water) just off the left bank two thirds of the way down. These lies are best addressed from the left bank. There are several other good pools below, the best of them being Pol na Trá, or Mahony's, where the river runs through a sharp (the rough water below an old ford), spreads into a deepish pool, and is then diverted into two streams. The fish lie on the far edge of the near stream, behind the rocks, and farther down under the trees. This run is also best fished from the near bank. We have usually stopped fishing at the big bend, because progress is obstructed by a drain and wire fences.

The river runs quickly from here to the town bridge, where it falls over rocks into a chain of big pools, which are tidal. The best of these is the Sea Pool, which was a highly rated pool in the past. It is more difficult to fish now in high summer because Sneem attracts a lot of visitors who make their way down here to look at the water.

The Sneem can produce twenty to thirty salmon to the lodge in a good year, almost all of them summer fish from the home beats. This figure would certainly be increased if all the river were fished in a more concentrated way over the season. This kind of lodge fishing, more domestic than the rather masculine sporting preserves such as Maxwell's Croy Lodge, is to be cherished; there are not large numbers of fish to be caught, but there are miles of good river to walk and fish, there are sporting sea-trout, and small browns in the hill loughs, and there is freedom from the meretricious fads of the organised holiday.

CHAPTER 6

The Erriff

July is the peak month of the year for one of the most sporting Irish fish, the grilse, and the loveliest place to fish for them is in the environment of the spate river. My favourite of these is the Erriff, in County Mayo.

The approach to the Erriff, from Leenaun, takes you along a winding road, not much more than a ledge, beside Killary harbour. The harbour is a fjord, a narrow, very deep estuary with sheer sides gouged out by glaciers. The same ice packs sculpted the dramatic contours of the Erriff valley, so that the river below Erriff bridge is hemmed in by mountains – Maumtrasna, Ben Gorm, the Devilsmother – which are constantly shadowed by the western cloudscapes.

Before checking in at the lodge, most anglers head for the bridge at Aasleagh, turning left onto the Louisburgh road, then under the rhododendrons, and the tiers of Scots pines, over the narrow metal span, to get their first view of the Erriff at the falls. You usually hear a good spate before you see it, often as you walk down the steep path through the pines from the lodge to the river. But at Aasleagh there is a grand view upstream from the bridge, to broad falls framed by the steep slopes of the valley. The falls are over fifty yards wide and twenty feet high, and pour into several streams, which are trained into channels between lines of boulders, converging to a single course just above the bridge.

In July, even with just a small spate chattering down between the rocks, a watcher at the bridge does not have long to wait before seeing grilse. They make deceptively small splashes, often in the smooth water just above a lip, sometimes in the rough channels. It is a sign of sport to come, because the smallest rise of water is propitious at the beginning of a week.

I have always arrived at Aasleagh Lodge on the afternoon before my first day. Not a second of a spate can be missed. That small freshet you saw at the bridge may be the last fresh water of the week. Grilse in a spate stream, as I will explain, are fish for the opportunist. Your only chance of one may depend on knowing just the time to be in the right place. Of course, if you arrive early and see good water, but cannot wet a line until after dinner, then the wait is a purgatory.

So with barely controlled impatience, or maybe in despair, you retrace your way back over the bridge, and then past the handsome inscribed stone at the gates, on to the lodge. It is, appropriately, a Victorian sporting lodge. From the terrace there is a view away to the west, up Killary harbour. The river is just below and when you are allocated Beat Nine you may take your rod from the rack and within a minute be putting a fly in front of grilse. Before then there is

63

acquaintance to renew, with Jim Stafford, the fishery manager, and his wife Mary, and the other rods who fish the river every year at the start of the grilse run.

*   *   *

The Erriff is over twenty miles long, but the prime fishing, in numbered beats, is on the bottom eight miles or so. Beat Nine, below Aasleagh falls, is streamy, rocky, and runs down quickly – just what is conjured up by the term spate river. The eight beats above (really above the Coronation Pool, the lowest pool on Beat Eight, which is structurally part of the Falls), are quite different. All are over a mile long and consist of runs, wide glides which can reduce to the thinnest water barely covering the gravels, and pools. The fast water looks the most inviting, but on the Erriff it is the slow, even dull, pools which hold the most fish. If I were given a choice of beat, Beat Two would be first, and of that beat, I would fish only the slow pools, above and including the Quarry Pool. Some people, indeed friends I have fished with on the Erriff, do not like this kind of river. They want the classic brimming, surging spate stream, with small balls of froth riding the dropping water. I like these too; I like all spate river fishing, but I love the Erriff, and its wide slow reaches, places like the Boat Pool on Beat Five, or the Dog Pool on Beat Two.

This is a typical holding pool on the river. It widens out, stretching about forty yards from bank to bank, immediately below the neck. The banks are peat, with vivid green grass and a sharp lip that drops down to the water's edge, to rushes and water lilies. The only perceptible current, even in high water, is at the neck and the tail. Beat Two holds fish from the earliest months of the Erriff year, so that one may get spring salmon there after April. A couple of years ago, in May, Anthony Luke took three fish over ten pounds in a day from this stretch. So if you wait long enough, you will almost always see fish on the Dog Pool, or if not there on one of the very similar adjacent pools, the Quarry Pool or the Road Reach.

The best fishing days on the Erriff are often recorded on these pools, but usually only when conditions are right. Received opinion has it that a spate river fishes best immediately after a spate. Not so the Erriff. A spate is often needed to bring salmon in, but you can fish the Erriff on a good falling water, in July, with grilse newly settled, and not stir a fin. This happens when the depression which has brought the rain and fish gives way to an anticyclone, with high blue skies and still airs. I hate this weather because it cheats you when so much has been promised. I have often found grilse reluctant takers in such conditions.

Compare this with what townsfolk call miserable weather; low but well-defined cloud, spots of rain, and a strong, warm south-westerly wind; twenty-five to thirty miles an hour is not too much. The narrow Erriff valley funnels the blast straight upstream and puts a rollicking wave on the wide pools. Now, when fresh fish are in, the Quarry Pool, the Dog Pool, the Black Banks, the Yellow Banks, the Boat Pool, and many others, can give the fishing of a lifetime. It will not be comfortable, and casting is trying. But a big wave on grey water makes the salmon eager, and it is sufficient to get a line out as best you can. They will take a fly savagely on such days.

Ideal conditions are rare, which is why the opportunism I mentioned earlier is the most important attribute of the spate river fly-fisher. As long as you remember a few points, it is often possible to extract a grilse in unpromising conditions. The first thing to note is that on slow pools a broken surface is vital. If you have found fish, and this is easy, especially when they are freshly arrived and roll a lot, then you must watch where they lie and fish there when a wind puts a ripple on the surface. I fished Beat Two with a friend, Les, in July, some years back, on a still hot day. Zephyrs came and went, in that irritating way that ruffles the water darkly in the distance, but which has dispersed to a calm when you come to it. We ran after the breezes all morning. After lunch we separated and I strolled up to the neck of the Dog Pool. I knew there were fish here, because I had seen them show earlier, and I waited for a ripple. When it came it pushed against the faint current running in at the neck and riffled the water there. I cast across it a few times, pulling in the flies, a Fiery Brown and a Silver Rat, yard by yard. About the third cast I though I felt a pluck, so I quickly threw out again to the same spot, and saw a fish turn at the fly. The next time it came over him the line went tight and I was into a grilse. By the time I had landed him, the breeze had died, and with it the fishing for the time being. We wandered about the pools until half past five, when we found ourselves back at the neck of the Dog, with the wind strengthening again. And as it did so, the

River Erriff. Beat Nine, Aasleagh Falls.

fish revived, so that I was into another one, from the same spot, almost immediately. It ran out the whole fly line, and thrashed in a small bay on the opposite bank, its back half out of water. I eased it in and played it out at my feet. While I was unhooking it, Les got into one, in exactly the same place; at six pounds it was the best of the afternoon.

Those three fish, from the same lie, were caught only because we fished over them while a fitful wind rippled the water. It did so for less than an hour or so, all told, during the entire (fishing) day of 6 July 1993, and gave us our main, perhaps only, chance of salmon that day. There is one other opportunity on a glassy surface in calm , bright weather, but only when grilse are fresh. That is when you can get a fly, immediately, to the very rings of a rise where a fish has rolled. He will sometimes take if you are quick enough.

Of course there are some lovely streams on the Erriff, and a great deal of the fast white water is found on Beat Nine. I am a convert to Beat Nine. In the early days I loathed it. Anglers are not the only ones to pause and look at Aasleagh Falls; every tour bus in Connemara seems to stop there, and to unload visitors who regard anglers as part of the local colour, to be pictured, or stood beside, or evenly frankly and loudly appraised, like any tourist prop. Also, at first glance this is a small beat, whose fishable pools and runs are quickly exhausted. This is to miss much of the subtlety of the beat.

Beat Nine consists of a number of runs. The main one leads from the salmon ladder, through the Garden Pools, down to the Gauge Pool. From mid-June this is one of the best series of pools on the river and often full of fish. It faces north, with a high bank and overhanging trees behind, so there is shade almost all day, and plenty of cover. It can be fished in the conventional way by swinging a wet-fly across it; this catches lots of fish. But for real excitement, this is first class water for the dibbled fly. A long, light rod, about fourteen foot, is needed. A bushy fly is attached to a dropper. Floatibility rather than pattern is important, so a small plastic tube, with a deer-hair collar and a long wing of light hair, is just the thing. A further eight feet down the leader, tie on a small bright fly, perhaps a Silver Rat. Let out just enough line to allow the dropper to touch the water, and no more; if you need to cast you are generally fishing too far away, and you will lose control. Now let the dropper play in the surface, in or just off the main runs of current. If there are fish about they will soon show, either breaking the water or turning under the dropper. I have risen over ten in a morning on the Garden Pool, fishing like this, but I had only two takes, and landed one fish, which took the point fly after turning away from the dropper, and those would not be untypical returns for the dibbled fly.

Exactly the same tactics can be used on the far (right) bank, fishing into the Falls Pool. It is best to fish from the big rocks, and to be shod with studded boots for a secure purchase while doing so. One can move right around, eventually casting upstream into the undertow of the pool. This fishes best, I find, a little later than the Garden Pools, and comes into its own in July. There are lots of other runs, upstream, where the dibbled fly can be used to the same effect. Wanklyn's Dam on Beat Seven is such a place, but you need to cross the near stream, and position yourself on the big grassy rock overlooking the main current, to get the best of it. The fly can be worked to a nicety here, and because of the angle of light you can see every move to it. Again, though, there are usually far more offers or rises, than firm takes.

The tides have a critical influence on Beat Nine. At high tide there is always a chance of fish at the Bridge and Sea Pools, so it pays to know your tide tables. In really low water, such as we had during the scorching summer of 1995, often the best, indeed the only realistic chance, of a fish on the whole river, was on Beat Nine, during high tide. The tourists are still a nuisance, especially on a fine day, but the attentive angler can ignore them and get fish if he knows his business.

Beat Nine is an education in how much there is to learn about a spate river before you can say you know it well. If it takes ten years to learn the secrets of a classic salmon beat, it will take a similar time to know the ways of fish in a relatively small river like the Erriff.

An experienced Erriff angler approaches each run and pool with a plan of attack in mind. The bank of vantage may change (beats on the river are double bank, and it is easily waded except in the highest water) several times as one works down the river. On Beat Seven, the upper part, including the Otter Pool and Wanklyn's Dam, is fished from the left bank; further down the Twin Rocks and the Sally Bush are also best addressed from the left bank. But the water beyond, down to the bend, holds fish towards the right bank so, after fishing the Sally Pool, a canny angler will go back upstream to the shallow glide, wade across there, and make his way downriver through the ferns and across the drains, almost to the bend. The casting is tricky, but it is much easier to reach the fish from here.

In some places the fish lie right under the near bank and are approached from there, but the angler while casting remains several feet inland. The Erriff fisher builds up a stock of such little stratagems with each year of experience.

*   *   *

The Erriff is nowadays mainly a grilse and summer salmon river. There are spring fish, but not many, although it must be said that relatively few rods fish for them. Jimmy Keogh, for the past few seasons, has had the first Erriff fish of the year, around Easter. The main run arrives at the end of June or beginning of July. They come in numbers and run up and down the tides of Killary until there is enough fresh water to bring them in. They do not need much. One can stand by the Garden Pool on Beat Nine, and see the constant flash of salmon running in streams only a couple of feet deep.

On some days in these weeks the twenty-five rods on the river may average a fish each, and sustained good conditions can produce weekly totals of over a hundred fish. All of these are grilse up to seven pounds and averaging three to four pounds. There are also some very small fish amongst them; I have had a grilse of less than a pound, and seen several others. When large numbers of fish are just in, the best taking days are often in relatively low water conditions, but with overcast skies and rough winds. Saturday 3 July 1993 was just such a day, when despite the low water the grilse were running strongly, and over twenty fish were caught.

Low water on Beat Three, the Erriff.

At the very beginning of this period, from about mid-June, the upper beats fill with salmon and Beat Nine holds pausing fish. Some of the lower beats sometimes seem not to hold much stock until July, but then they can offer bumper days. I have fished Beats Seven and Eight, both wonderful beats, in mid-June, and have seen very few fish while upstream plenty were showing. A couple of weeks, or even days later, and no amount of bribery would persuade a rod on Beat Eight to swap for an upper beat; I have seen a man come away with six in a day from Beat Eight in early July.

From mid-July the fishing settles down into the familiar spate river rhythm, of flood and famine. All the summer months, into September, can give excellent fishing if the water is right. Good water might last a day, not usually much more. As an example take Tuesday 3 August 1993. Tony and I arrived in the afternoon, just as a good spate was slowly running down. We had the frustration of standing at Aasleagh, seeing lovely water, and being unable to fish until after dinner. It was doubly unfortunate because a rare conjunction of conditions had brought heavy rain and a big rise in the river level the previous day, then supplemental rain overnight, which allowed the river to fall ever so slowly. Over twenty salmon were

6lb grilse from the Erriff.

taken that day, including six by one rod on Beat Six (he lost four others). I hooked and lost a fish on Beat Four after dinner, in the gloaming, and that was it for the evening. The next day, the river had fallen away, the sun was bright, and the planets moved into other orbits. I toiled for hours until, on my umpteenth pass through the lovely run at the head of the Washing Pool, I hooked a very tough five pound fish. That was one of only six salmon caught during the day.

*   *   *

In July a single-handed rod is by far the best tool for much of the good water on the Erriff. The slack pools are fished as you would fish a stillwater, that is cast, retrieve in slow pulls of a yard or so, cast at a different angle. A longish line is often an advantage to cover as much of the width of the river as possible. There are the pools I have mentioned on Beat Two, but there are also the Black Banks on Beat Six, the Broken Bridge, Yellow Banks, and the Boat Pool on Beat Five, the Otter Pool and the lower Sally Pool on Beat Seven, among many others, which are often more than forty yards wide and where the competent caster will cover more fish. To get the best from the Erriff, a rod must master the wind, which can rise from a fairly comfortable fifteen mile an hour breeze to blasts funnelled up Killary and the narrow and deep Erriff valley, bringing stinging rain and sending you stumbling over the turf.

I have used a number of rods to cope with Atlantic weather, and I have arrived at a nine foot, fast-action rod (a Sage RPL), carrying a number seven forward taper floating line. When the wind really blows, a slow-sinker, because of its slim profile, is better. This outfit throws a fast narrow loop, which is the only hope of getting any distance when your coat is flapping like washing on a line. For dibbling a long double handed rod, as light as you can get, is wanted.

Most Erriff regulars swear by small flies. From June a number ten would be about the standard size, but a twelve is also useful in thin water. A bigger hook may be used in the lower beats, especially Beat Nine, when really fresh salmon are the quarry, than on the upper beats where fish may have been in fresh water for longer. Of course, as the summer wears on and the fish become stale, a very small hook may sometimes be the only choice. I do most of my Erriff fishing in June and July, so I much prefer a single hook in sizes ten and twelve, and my favourite pattern for spate river fishing is the Partridge Salmon Iron. It has a good gape and a strong wire, both essential. Singles have served me at least as well as trebles for this fishing – that is, I am certain they hold as securely, if not more so. I have never suffered a really searing loss with a single, although I have had fish up to fifteen pounds work loose from an apparently secure connection with a number six treble. A particular advantage of singles on this river, where a great deal of work is done with single-handed rods and longish lines, is that they are not quite so dangerous flying about your head. If I were to use flies consistently smaller than size twelves I would probably turn to a treble for notional security but, as I rarely use these small hooks on the Erriff, the single pattern I mention serves me for most of the time.

The fishing record at the lodge shows a confusing array of patterns. I keep them fairly simple. Jim Stafford strongly advises a Black Pennell for his river, and I have done well by following it. The Black Pennell would be my first choice for a dropper. For the point, silvery flies, like the Silver Rat, do well on Beats Eight and Nine. Upriver, where the water is stained dark by peat, some of the older patterns winged with hair instead of feather are good. Sidney Spencer fished a great deal for salmon on loughs and swore by the Fiery Brown for peat-stained water, so I follow that counsel, and it has given me fish.

*   *   *

The Erriff was, like many of the small rivers in the west, owned in its entirety by one proprietor, in this case the Marquis of Sligo. The lower valley, below Erriff bridge, is now sparsely inhabited, and there are few signs of earlier settlement. Only the odd ruined cottage, and drystone sheepfolds, remain. There are also lazy beds, tiny plots of small parallel embankments perhaps a foot high and two feet wide, the relics of despairing efforts in the nineteenth century to provide a topsoil which would support the staple potato crop in a barren terrain suited only to pasturage. However poor the land, rights over it were strongly asserted, and there is still melancholy evidence of this driven existence in the drystone walls, threading up almost perpendicular slopes towards ridges two thousand feet high, desperately differentiating one impoverished holding from its neighbour.

In this century, the river was leased by individuals, but management was difficult, and the annual take of salmon was small. Grimble, in his *Salmon Rivers of Ireland*, written in 1913, is dismissive of it, condemning it as a stream which runs down too quickly to be of note as a salmon fishery; he recommends brown trout fishing in nearby loughs, which is bizarre advice. I wonder how much he actually knew of it. Certainly attempts had been made to cultivate the fishery. A fairly large hatchery system was built, and a fish pass installed to allow salmon to negotiate the almost impassable barrier of Aasleagh Falls.

The Central Fisheries Board acquired both the fishing rights on the river, and Aasleagh Lodge, in the early 1980s, and this single fact is responsible for the flourishing river we see today. It had suffered badly from poaching, and this was stopped, largely due to the efforts of Fishery Board staff. Estuarial netting was also brought under control. Formerly, the boats had been able to follow fish up the narrow Killary Harbour as far as the Tidal Pool. When, as often happens, there was no water, and the fish dropped back with the ebbing tide, they were completely at the mercy of the netsmen. Nowadays, the nets have to observe a rule that they do not net within a certain distance of the river mouth.

The redds were watched at spawning times. Banks were shored up, because the river winds through strata of peat and soft glacial deposits which erode easily. Stiles and access points were improved. And, as important, the necessary work was done with discretion, to preserve the traditional landscape.

Since the take-over, the annual catch has improved steadily, from about two hundred fish in the early 1980s to over eight hundred fish in recent years. (Grimble, in 1913, thought it worth mentioning that a rod had once taken five fish off the river in a day; nowadays, it happens several times a season.) This is an excellent return from a river which has a short effective season, from about mid-June to the end of September.

*   *   *

The Erriff has a sound management regime. A strong feature of it is that rods which are resident at Aasleagh Lodge may, at the manager's discretion, which is only rarely refused, go after dinner to the beat allocated for the next day, and also fish there before breakfast of the same day. So, of an evening, unless the water is dead low, as soon as Jim pins up on the dining room mantelpiece the beat allocations for the morrow, most rods are off to the river.

These hours at dusk are invaluable if there is a falling water, but also, in low water, they may be the best time of day for rousing fish which have become stale and difficult. Similarly, early morning can be good, though not, I have found, as good as the evening. Still, I have reason to be glad of getting out before breakfast; one morning, at the Sally Pool on Beat Seven, I hooked a ten pound fish at half past seven, and played it for ten minutes before landing it. I fished on after breakfast, but that was my only take of the day.

The detail of such a struggle remains long in the memory, and the recall of this good fish coming up to the surface, then with a wave of its body going deep and pulling the rod over, with me stumbling down the bank after it, still holds a charge. Behind such episodes there persist abiding memories of the valley, of the lumpy, glinting sides of Maumtrasna, of the folds of mountains receding into infinity on the western skyline, and the freshness of the long wind from the Atlantic. The companionship of the lodge, of familiar faces seen every year over the dinner table, is one pleasure of the Erriff. A more profound one is absorbed when you walk, alone, beside the quiet river, a solitary figure in that landscape.

Above: Upstream wind on Junction Pool, the Owenduff.
Below: River Erriff, Beat Nine, Bridge Pool.

CHAPTER 7

Salmon Fishing on the Loughs

The road to Burrishoole dips and swerves into the Nephin Beg range, along the valley made by the loughs – Feeagh and Furnace – which constitute the fishery. I approached it on the morning of 18 July, in a year when all the west of Ireland had experienced long weeks of drought, with low water in river and lough and the year's crop of grilse running up and down the tides of estuaries at the mercy of the netsmen. Overnight there had been steady though light rain, and I was pleased to see that it had put a flush into the Mill Race, which was showing some white water. I was to fish with John, one of the young Furnace gillies, that day, and he suggested that we have a few casts in the Mill Race to start off.

This is a narrow stream, only ten feet wide, flowing between rocky sides out into the lough. The received wisdom is that when there is a good fresh in it, the salmon gather around the outflow and if seen are usually takers. Well, we saw lots in the hour that we fished, but did not have a pull. They rolled near the fly, and flashed under it, continuously. But later that day, after lunch, one of the rods hooked a big fish here which played deep for over five minutes, and ran from one side of the flow to the other, until finally it snagged the dropper on one of the rocks.

There was a big run of salmon in, and all the usual rules were being turned on their heads. Fish can easily move into Furnace on the high tides, and the stock in the lough (an estimated two thousand salmon) was due entirely to this, because there had been no rain of any account for months. High spring tides had helped the influx of fish, and made the waters of Furnace, which are always slightly saline, more brackish. Traditionally, this has put salmon off the take, but not in this year; the fishing was the best in recent memory; on one day in the week ending 16 July, nine boats had twenty-nine grilse. The total for the week was 120 grilse for 141 rod days.

The morning was perfect for salmon fishing from a boat, so we soon headed down to the Yellow River Bay. The south-westerly wind put a good wave on the lough but was soft in your face, and still had a salt tang from the waters of Clew Bay, just a few miles to the south west. Low cloud swung over from the west in clearly defined ranks. I pray for days like this, and I would always have them instead of the days of high cloud and bright passages which many Irish writers of the past favoured. A warm, close day, with a good south-westerly wind, is as near the ideal as one will get on a lough. John turned the boat broadside at Duffy's Point, and trimmed it so that I was casting into the rocky shore, mere yards from the breaking waves. I fished a Green Peter on the dropper (a fly which I had never liked until that day, but which has done well down the years at Burrishoole), and a small shrimp fly on the point. The boat rode a lovely wave, the wind blew nicely, and downwind, salmon turned or jumped; the angler who has fished in all the unfavourable combinations of wind or weather which is his usual lot will fall into a tense concentration at such times. I was not surprised, when, less than half an hour after starting, I had a strong take underwater to the point fly, and the fish was firmly hooked. It was a very small grilse, a wild fish which anglers on Burrishoole are now encouraged to return.

We fished that first drift right into the sandy bottom of the bay around the inflow of the Yellow River, and though we stirred more fish, and had some half-takes, nothing more decisive happened. This lough is tidal, and we were fishing on the height of the flood, so that a nest of rocks in mid-bay were covered and we could float over them, as we did on our second drift. A fish dashed from the rocks, and took the Green Peter in a swirl, then ran out a good length of line behind the boat. It also ran out of ideas, and spent a few minutes seeking shelter under the keel. Such fish, especially in shallow water, create special difficulties, because they seem to yield completely, but then dash away in fright, and the alternating pressures on the hook hold sometimes cause it to slip. However, we landed this one, but returned it immediately as it was a sea-trout, a good fish over two pounds. We had seen several salmon move on the line of drift, so we went back to the head and came down again, and this time I had a strong pull from a grilse of three or four pounds, on the point fly, which ran away to my right but then slipped loose.

We then continued down on this drift, towards Fahy's Angle. Pastures incline steeply towards the lough in this quarter, and are retained by unique drystone walls with their lower courses in the water; piers of rough granite blocks, assembled by farmers last century, project into the lough, and we fished past these down to a corner where a line of stakes running out into the water made an angle with the stony shore. The surface here was quiet; I had begun to fish passively when a great boil surrounded the Green Peter, and a salmon was on. John immediately began to back the boat into open water. Fortunately the fish ran back upwind, instead of down through the stakes and took out the whole line. It then swung across, and came to the top, jumping clear several times above the heavy chop. I got it back near the boat, where it bored in circles, and then lay on its side and fell into the net. It was a typical Furnace fish of five and a half pounds, full of spirit and dash, and the most sporting fish that can be taken from a boat on the Irish loughs. Sea-trout would be their equal, but they rarely grow to this size in the west, except for those of Lough Currane. Brown trout are strong, but not nearly as wild fighters as these grilse, when fresh, in shallow water. We unhooked the salmon and went back for lunch.

It had been a good morning, with a sweet wind, fish moving, and two grilse plus a handsome sea-trout in the boat. We expected more sport in the afternoon, but in the west the weather shifts are sudden and complete. During lunch, the wind had swept all the cloud from the sky, and we were covered by bright blue wastes for the whole afternoon; the wind kept up, but the wave was glittering with spangled light, a condition I hate for lough salmon, and we did not stir a fin.

The Burrishoole fishery is run by the Salmon Research Agency of Ireland, in conjunction with its research and development work in salmonids and commercial smolt rearing. The salmon fishery comprises Lough Feeagh, a large lough two and a half miles long, which runs into Lough Furnace. Furnace discharges almost directly into its estuary, and is itself tidal. This partly explains the quality of the fishing in dry summers. Salmon do not need a flood to run into Furnace, they just come in on the tides. Consequently this lough is regularly replenished with fresh stocks when other waters in the west are barren in times of low water. In dry summers such as the one just described, the fishing at Burrishoole can be largely confined to Furnace; neither the Mill Race nor the Salmon Leap run heavily enough to encourage many fish to continue their journey up to Feeagh. But salmon usually spread out through the whole fishery, and Feeagh holds a large stock of fish.

The season at Burrishoole extends from 10 June to the end of September, and is now almost exclusively a grilse season, although there are also good quality sea-trout. There were spring salmon here, and the remains of stone-built draft netting stations, at the Black Rock on Furnace, show their commercial importance. Unfortunately the netting, decades ago, was too successful, and it is feared that the loughs' run of spring salmon may have been lost. Historically, the Burrishoole loughs were valued mainly as sea-trout fisheries. Grimble (*Salmon Rivers of Ireland*) , in 1913, mentioned only the sea-trout ('baskets of from half a dozen to three dozen may be made here in moist weather during July and August'). However, the 1928 edition of *Where to Fish* noted that Feeagh was the best angling lake in the district for salmon and sea-trout, a significant claim since the district would have included Loughs Beltra and Carrowmore. It also noted that anglers coming to these loughs sometimes used flies which were too big, and this point is still valid.

The fishing on these loughs is mainly by boat, although there is some bank fishing on Furnace, in the Mill Race at the management's discretion, at the Back Weir, and for tidal sessions at the Neck when the fish are holding there.

Burrishoole salmon are affected by both spates of fresh water, and tidal influences. Spates encourage fish to move through the system, but they also dilute the amount of salt water in Furnace, and traditionally this has had a marked effect on the fishing. During spring tides, especially in dry spells, it was received knowledge that the high salt content of the water discouraged the take in Furnace, but in the summer I described earlier, in exactly those conditions, boats came in with big bags of fish. It is suspected that the number of fish running, increased perhaps by the lifting of Greenland and Faroese nets, may have had an effect.

The lies on the loughs, especially on Furnace, seem to alter from season to season. In some seasons a lot of fish hold in the Neck, or perhaps around the Salmon Leap, the main run into Feeagh. In other years, many salmon are taken in the Yellow River Bay and Fahy's Angle, but the Salmon Leap, Rusheen and Blacksod Bay can also hold plenty of fish. They can lie right in by the bank in two feet of water; I have risen fish in that depth of water, with hardly a ripple on it, in Blacksod Bay. The lies on Feeagh are rather more predictable, and a number centre on the mouths of streams flowing into the lough.

With adequate water, both Furnace and Feeagh have good stocks of fish and there are only nine boats fishing, four or five on each. This allows great freedom of drifts, given that Feeagh is over two miles long and a half a mile wide, and Furnace itself is a substantial lough. Boats can be concentrated on Furnace in dry years, or when relatively few fish have run into Feeagh, but there is still plenty of room. Whereas Feeagh has a rather regular shape, the shoreline of Furnace loops into lots of little bays and inlets; there is plenty of the essential architecture of lough salmon lies – headlands, rocky shoals, stone piers – and acres of water in the critical three to seven feet range. I prefer Furnace because of this intimate scale and variety, but a good day on the wide spaces of Feeagh can change allegiances.

Both loughs get the full benefit of Atlantic breezes which come from just over the hills. The weather changes quickly here; I described earlier the first of two days which were typical. The next morning was similar to the first, and although we did not boat a salmon, both Pat Hughes, the fishery manager, and myself rose several fish, and landed some excellent sea-trout. We could not fish after lunch because the wind was gusting at more than thirty-five miles an hour and there were racing whitecaps all over the lough.

Lough Furnace, Burrishoole. Yellow River Bay.

The 1928 edition of *Where to Fish* commented about the small sizes of fly required at Burrishoole. I first came across this ten years ago, when Pat Hughes counselled us to use nothing larger than a size ten, or possibly an eight in rough weather. Most people still use small flies at Burrishoole, which is character-building when a number ten hook is your link to a wild fish threshing about in the surface twenty yards upwind. Relatively fine long leaders, above ten pound test, are also favoured. A selection of traditional patterns – Claret Bumble, Green Peter, Bibio, Invicta – on strong size eight and ten singles, are required for Burrishoole. The Bibio has special local associations because it was created for the Burrishoole loughs by Major Roberts. Other patterns which have recently done well are the Green Highlander, the Clan Chief, and small shrimp patterns. Ken Whelan showed me some Canadian flies, mainly Green Butts, which he finds effective; he also revealed another Canadian fly, a large pink thing, which only a fishery director could possibly get away with using; I could not see a gillie allowing me to bring one into the boat.

*   *   *

Fly-fishing for lough salmon is one of the rarest pleasures of the game fisher's year. Good river fly-fishing, in contrast, is relatively easily got. With careful management, however, the salmon angler on the Irish loughs can have continuous angling through the year. Although lough fishing for salmon begins in Ireland in January on the lakes of Killarney, this is almost exclusively trolling, and while productive it is not the most interesting angling. For the fly-fisher, the year starts in February. Spring fishing is excellent on the Delphi fishery in

County Mayo, where adventurous management has boosted the spring run dramatically. It is true that many Delphi springers come off the beautiful Bundorragha river, but some are caught on fly from Finlough.

Lough Carrowmore also opens in February. This lough is part of the Owenmore system, and while later in the year summer fish run straight up the river, spring salmon tend to run into the lough. It can be extremely productive – I know of a local angler who had over thirty spring salmon on the fly in the 1995 season (which was an exceptionally good one). Carrowmore is distinguished by two features. It can have long quiet spells, when it seems there is not a salmon within miles although the keel of a drifting boat will have gone over dozens. The fishing is also highly influenced by the wind; the lough is shallow and has a very silty bottom. A big blow stirs up the sediment and puts off the salmon until everything settles again.

Lough Beltra, which opens in the second week of March, is almost exclusively a spring salmon lough, whose runs of fish have held up well in recent years as the sea-trout fishery here has declined. The experience of Anthony Gourlay, of Glamorgan, in the 1996 season, shows how good this fishing can be. He met salmon on every one of the five days he fished at the start of the season, bagging at least one fish a day; in the middle of this spell, he took two in a day, one in the morning and one in the afternoon. The extraordinary feature of this angling is that while salmon fisherman on rivers are using sunk lines and big heavy flies at this time, the fish of Beltra are coming to flies no larger than size ten, fished in the very top of the water. All Anthony Gourlay's fish took a dibbled dropper. The method, and the tackle, are hardly distinguishable from those used in July.

Fishing on Beltra and Carrowmore continues into April and May, when other loughs come into the reckoning. By late May Lough Melvin will have had a good run of grilse, which will have run through the lough as far as the Rossinver fishery. By mid-June other runs of grilse should be appearing, and a range of loughs then become attractive options. Screebe will have had some fish in from early spring, but a good run should be about to come in around the time of the longest day. Burrishoole will be getting its main stock of grilse then. The Kylemore loughs have steadily improved in the last decade, and are definitely worth fishing in June and July; of these the best is the biggest lough, Kylemore. The Costello and Fermoyle fishery has both lough and river fishing. It gets a run of big summer fish, some of them over twenty pounds, and the best shaped salmon in Connemara. If you hit it right, fishing on the loughs of this system can be spectacular. They are quite distinct, but the choicest spot on any of them , for a salmon, must be the Butts of Fermoyle; here Pádraig McDonagh took five fish in a couple of hours one August evening in 1995, when wind and flood conspired to produce perfect conditions.

*   *   *

Fishing for salmon from a drifting boat is highly specialised, and there is much to learn: about boat-handling; about the lies of fish and their behaviour in the highly variable water heights and weather conditions of Atlantic seaboard fisheries; about flies and fishing tactics. The best writing on Irish lough fishing for salmon is contained in Sidney Spencer's books, although they also cover the Hebridean waters that he loved. Spencer fished mainly in Donegal, in Lough Eske and Lough Beagh, and a lot of his fishing there was done in spring, in the days when the spring run was still a significant part of the sporting calendar. If you want to know what it was like to fish a lough on wild, raw days, and to battle with big salmon using a short rod and steel wrists, read his essays; they are incomparable. (A number of them were recently re-printed under the title *Fishing the Wilder Shores*).

Salmon tend to gather around inflow streams (hence the importance of fishing stands on the Butts of these western loughs), near the rocky shoals, headlands, and structures such as piers, mentioned earlier with regard to Lough Furnace. However, not all such places will ever hold fish, nor will many of them host numbers of salmon all the time. As ever, local knowledge is crucial. They should be fished with the greatest care, and Spencer was particularly insistent that a salmon lie was almost always best approached form a boat drifting from deeper to shallower water.

An angler straight from the trout loughs, where fish are more widely distributed, and whose dispersal is affected anyway by the scatter of a fly hatch, is often content to let the boat drift where the wind will take it in the general areas of lies. This is not the way to fish them. The boat needs to be managed by a boatman with good nerve, whose oars softly stroke the water. Lies have to be fished quietly but thoroughly, so the direction of the boat's drift must be closely managed; it is useless to be driven across a corner of a lie quickly and helplessly in front of the wind. When the lies can vary from year to year the boatman's knowledge is vital. Boat management is also essential when one hooks a lively fish in shallow water, especially in lies near rough shorelines and obstructions like stone piers. Salmon fly-fishing from a boat is a partnership, and an equal partnership at that, between angler and boatman.

Spencer used tackle which would feel a bit heavy for us now. I know, because on our first day on the Screebe loughs, my friend had brought with him a ten foot long (steel-centred) Hardy's Gold Medal. It was a rod for an heroic age, when anglers could wield such eight or ten ounce single-handed rods all day. We are fortunate in having a wider choice of longer, much lighter, weapons, and this is a particular boon for the salmon angler on stillwater because of the importance of the bobbed fly in bringing up, if not hooking, fish. The most striking initial difference between river and lough fishing is the number of salmon that you rise in the summer months; it is nothing unusual to see a dozen or more fish come up to look at the flies in the course of a fishing day. I remember a morning on the Salmon Leap at Burrishoole when I had that number of enquiries in a couple of hours. Fish swirled at the fly, or just appeared behind it, their dorsals and tails cutting the surface. I hooked none of them but, if I could have managed another foot of draw, one would have felt the steel, because he made up his mind to take just as I lifted off, and he turned, open-mouthed, at the spot the fly had just left. It is the dropper, furrowing along the surface, which is chiefly responsible. The longer that the dropper can be made to work like this, the more interest you will arouse. And other things being equal, the longer your rod, the longer the draw. A light eleven foot carbon, thin in section, is therefore the weapon of choice for lough salmon fishing from a boat. Diameter is important because good conditions mean a strong wind at your back, and lifting a thick sectioned rod against this, no matter what its weight on the scales, quickly saps your strength. The rod should be a good roll-caster, because a lot of false casting is bad technique for the close-quarter fishing you do from a boat. A long line is rarely necessary. Ten yards of fly line, rolled forward, first drawn by hand then lifted to trip the dropper before rolling forward again at the end of the lift, is sufficient. This easy fluency of style is also much less fatiguing over a day's fishing.

Design of the flies, rather than pattern, determines their position on the leader. The dropper obviously needs to be a bulky dressing, so flies with palmered bodies are the norm. Spencer favoured specific patterns for certain conditions of light, but I am not convinced. I would happily fish any bushy fly, in the right sizes, (a size ten as normal, up to an eight in a big wave) on the dropper, and a more streamlined design on the point. I feel that the point fly should be small, and I have always done best with slim shrimp dressings on size twelve trebles.

*   *   *

Southern Connemara, roughly the land south of a line between Oughterard and Clifden, and the sea, is a place of big skies and low hills. A litter of granite, in slabs and loose boulders, is cast over the thin peat and outcrops of bedrock. The narrow roads wind and bump over the hard terrain, intersecting at junctions where there is a confusion of signs in Irish (this is a Gaeltacht, where Irish is not just a nationalistic piety, but the natural first language) and English. There are few trees, little grass, and pale colours until in summer the blush of fuchsia lights up the drystone walls. The rock falls into the most involved coastline in Ireland, which on the map is a filigree of inlets and islands.

This landscape is partly what gives such character to a unique cluster of salmon and sea-trout fisheries here: Screebe, Costello and Fermoyle, Gowla and Invermore are all separate river/lough systems. The first two especially cover very large areas, yet the individual loughs of each system are quite distinct little jewels. There is nowhere else in Ireland like them, and you would need to go a long way to find a similar harmony of water and bog and rock.

The Salmon Pool on Screebe Lough is one of the great pools of Connemara, indeed of Irish salmon fishing. A small river runs in at the head, into a bay between the Butts, two arms of drystone piers. They are handsome nineteenth century structures, weathered to a permanence as impressive as that of the bare rock outcrops on the enfolding hills. I went down to Screebe Lough with Bob Hutchinson on a close July morning. Low cloud hung static overhead and only a faint breeze came in from the sea just to the south. We stored our gear in the little whitewashed Lunch Hut, the most comforting of its kind I have ever been in, and now after a century of existence a part of this unique landscape. The two lough boats were pulled up in the inlet outside and would hardly be used on this calm day.

I asked Bob to go ahead; I have fished long enough to know that in salmon angling the statement that ninety per cent of angling knowledge is local knowledge is particularly apt. Bob now guides anglers on Screebe but he has fished here for many years and when he was a paying guest he would get up to thirty salmon a year from the water. His opinions are worth attention. He went first to the nearest pier. It is three feet above the water and has a width of four

H-R Hebeisen playing a salmon on the Salmon Pool, Screebe.

feet, its blackened granite blocks as solid as bedrock. A good fishing wind, from points west, blows onto the left shoulder here, although it was light enough that morning. Bob fished each bit of water, from beside the pier to as far as he could cast, carefully but at a good pace, so that he moved steadily along and soon turned its corner, where it heads north towards the mouth of the river. He retrieved his flies in draws of a foot at a time, at a much faster lick than I have seen elsewhere, but it has worked for him. He fished two flies of his own devising, one of them the Lady Ethna, a very successful fly for fresh fish at Screebe. Both were dressed on the size twelve and fourteen trebles which he favours, and it is a fact that Screebe fish are generally caught on small flies.

Some choice fishing ground is addressed from this corner; it forms the mouth of the bay, and salmon which lie here, sometimes in hundreds, waiting to run the little river, show their back and tail fins in those easy rolls indicative of resting fish. Bob has seen them lie still with the mere points of their tails set like little sails in the surface. I had seen a few fish show as I watched Bob. I followed him out, casting a lengthening line, retrieving in short strokes, and had come within five yards of the corner of the pier when the line suddenly pulled away from me and a fish thrashed on top. This one was always ahead of the game. It ran out, then in and I had to hand-line quickly to catch up with it. Then it surged out again and all the loose line whipped off the rock at my feet after it. It jumped at the extremity of its run, tore to the left, and ran in to my feet. I had just caught up with the line cutting into the water five yards out from me, when I saw the fish swim in circles three feet down almost beside the pier. There was a slight catch, that terrible slackening in the line and in the nerves, and I felt hollow. It had been a good salmon of ten pounds or more. When I looked at the loose line, only a few inches of abraded nylon remained below the dropper. The fish had gone around a rock, and the ten pound material I was using had chafed away in a moment. Bob is a phlegmatic man, and when he offered me some of his fifteen pound nylon in a disinterested gesture I willingly took it. Later I was glad to have it.

The two arms of the piers on the Salmon Pool are only thirty yards apart at their widest, and the bay narrows to about five yards where the little river runs in. I saw Bob fishing this with particular care. I did not think he had much of a chance, because the breeze did not penetrate far into the bay, and a hot sun was coming out. But Bob knew what he was about and shouted to me as he hooked a fish in the apparently dead stillness of that water. There is a little thread of current below the bridge and a lie there where often two or three fish are at rest. Bob had raised one of these. It was a very unusual capture, because the salmon had taken the little fly deeply, and it penetrated a blood vessel in the gills causing it to bleed badly. It was almost dead when landed, but was still a lovely fish of over seven pounds, silver and sea-liced despite the fact that there had not been significant water in southern Connemara for weeks.

I loved Screebe at first sight, in September 1984, despite my day beginning with a cow eating the chrome trim from one side of my car, and ending with two of us coming away from the lough, beaten, after seeing tens of fish rising but not taking. It is a wild place with the unique southern Connemara harmony of low hills and rock. There is an intimacy in the landscape but it was a terrible country in which to eke a livelihood during the last century. Nowadays, ironically, it gives a special nourishment to minds distracted by the pressures of metropolitan life. It has an incomparable, austere beauty.

The great virtue of Screebe is that much of the system, right up to the Salmon Pool, is tidal. So the fish move in and out even in dry spells, when other rivers and loughs are low and empty. The morning I described followed a week of heatwave; Denise, my wife, and I had driven down to Galway the previous afternoon in a car which was hot even with the air rushing in through open windows. The sky curved blue out into Galway Bay and the meadows were parched brown. The following morning Bob caught that fresh silver fish despite not a drop of rain having fallen overnight. It was a true 'tidey', as fresh salmon used to be called in parts of Ireland long ago; a fish which had been in the system only a few days.

The Screebe system is big and intricate. It discharges into Camus Bay, through a narrow run which is very brackish. Tidal influences are very strong here and the levels rise and fall considerably with the ebb and flood. Salmon fishing in this salt water can be very good at the late stages of the ebb, a fact noted in Grimble (*The Salmon Rivers of Ireland*, 1913). There were three recognised stands in those days, and they have been restored and supplemented. They consist of piers which extend over the greasy rocks and bladderwrack, and have to be maintained by hard work each year. At the latter part of the ebb these command casting positions over fast streams of transparent water, where salmon show regularly; at least they did on the afternoon I fished there with Bob. But even though salmon in the sea will not always take in the bright hot weather we suffered that afternoon, it was an experience to fish for them with fly in a marine environment. These stands are now known by the collective name of the Road Pools and they are some of the most productive parts of the Screebe system. Above these are Glencoh and Derrywoniff (Loch an tSáile Íochtarach is the Irish name, meaning lough of the briny or saline water, south), both shallow loughs dotted with rocky islets. Neither is fished regularly as it is thought that fish do not lie in them, but this could change. Certainly salmon do lie at the top of Derrywoniff, where the incoming river flows alongside the Butts; this is an excellent stand for fish. The stream which links Derrywoniff with Screebe Lough (Loch an tSáile Thualdh) can also be good, especially with a wave on it; it is accessed by boat, usually from Screebe Lough.

Screebe Lough is the centrepiece of the fishery. The lower lough, below the island, was good for sea-trout (I saw a fair number of these fish, and caught several, during a recent three day stay). The salmon fishing is concentrated mainly in the upper lough, and unusually the drifts did not need to follow closely the shorelines or promontories, as is often the case in stillwater salmon fishing. Fish seem to lie everywhere in this shallow lough, although Pádraig, one of the boatman on Screebe Lough, told me that in some years he meets most of his fish near the shorelines.

There are two boats on Screebe Lough, allowing each a princely amount of space on a water which I would guess covers over a hundred acres. The boat fishing is the better for the fact that engines are not allowed on these loughs, for the practical reason that they are too shallow and rocky. They are also small

83

enough to make managing a boat by oars alone possible for a couple of anglers sound in wind and limb. I am sure that this lack of disturbance leads to more salmon being caught. I know from fishery managers on other loughs that there is a much better chance of a salmon early in the morning, even on fairly calm water, than later when the engines begin to plough furrows in the surface. It is a fact that many anglers are careless about motoring inside other boats' lines of drift, or in shallow fish-holding areas. One may also fish from the shore here, and there are a good number of fine stone piers on the northern and southern sides which offer excellent bank fishing – indeed the best bank fishing for lough salmon which I have seen in Ireland.

The Salmon Pool is a separate beat, distinguished from Screebe Lough beat by a group of three stones, inside which a boat cannot drift; it is exclusively bank fishing. Anglers fishing the Salmon Pool have the two great arms of the Butts as platforms, plus an extensive bank and a smaller pier on the northern shore. They also have the little stretch of river below the footbridge, at the neck of the Pool,

Playing a salmon, the Mill Race, Lough Furnace, Burrishoole.

in which salmon always seem to lie. To fish for them here, in water not five yards wide and only three feet deep is extraordinary.

The river winds from the Hatchery down to the Salmon Pool and forms another beat. It is extremely good in a high flood, but poor in low water. It has been widened a little, and lies have been created within its narrow banks in recent times, but it is still possibly the smallest genuine salmon river in Ireland. Only the Fane in County Louth can compare with it for size, and that river is generally wider and deeper. There is a complex network of loughs and streams in the plateau above, containing as much water as the system below the hatchery, but it is less fished. A lot of water is needed to bring salmon up, but when stocked, these are also splendid loughs.

The hatchery at Screebe is worth a visit. It is the second oldest hatchery in Ireland, after Oughterard, and has been enhancing the system's salmon stocks for over one hundred years. I went through the old fishing register (with entries going back to 1860) when I was last there and an entry in 1909, by the then lessee Howard St George, notes that the hatchery work was suspended in 1907–1908 to test whether natural recruitment was sufficient to maintain salmon stocks. Obviously it was thought not to be, because the hatchery work soon resumed, and has continued ever since. Screebe was then part of the Ballynahinch estate, and estate account books, now held at Screebe itemise netting and other costs associated with the hatchery.

The hatchery is now under the management of Ethna O' Brien, a woman of keen eye and sardonic wit, to whom you bring your salmon after capture, and who feelingly informs you if it was one of her hatchery babies. I brought her a six pound fish which indeed was one of her protégés and for a time, a very little time, I felt a slight guilt. I was soon happy again, however, because after losing a good fish, and not meeting another for a day, to get one on my last day was a relief in a season in which I had lost more salmon than I had landed. There is good reason for asserting that the sporting health of the Screebe estate depends on Ethna's work at the hatchery.

The returns of salmon to Screebe and Burrishoole these days comprise a high proportion of ranched fish, originating from smolts propagated at the respective hatcheries. Ranched fish are recognised by a clipped adipose fin. They also contain a minute nose tag, implanted in the smolts. This nose tag is removed from captured fish, and a flesh sample taken, for analysis. Burrishoole is attempting to increase the proportion of wild grilse by making their release compulsory from August, and compensating the anglers concerned with a ranched fish; not enough ranched fish are being cropped at present.

The efforts, and the rewards now being experienced at Screebe, Burrishoole, Costello and Delphi confirm that salmon stock enhancement and ranching is necessary work for many Galway and Mayo fisheries. If the activities of drift nets, and predation by seals, could be controlled, these fisheries would be even more important to Ireland's sporting economy. There is evidence that drift nets do damage not only by the salmon landed, but also by the salmon which seals take from them. Some estimates put drift net landings at between ten and fifty per cent of fish originally trapped – the seals take the rest .

The Screebe fishing register is one of the most interesting of Irish sporting records, and it is of more general note because it contains not only the details of Howard St George's tenancy of the fishery, from 1896 to 1913, but also the records of his subsequent fishing on the best salmon waters of the time. Seasonal totals from Screebe varied between about fifty fish in poor years to over one hundred and fifty in good years, such as 1903, to approximately three rods. It was in this year, on the 30 June, that St George took eighteen fish in a day, eight before midday. The fact is recorded with cheerful inaccuracy in George Cornwallis-West's *Edwardians Go Fishing* (1932), which includes some pages of description of Screebe; he has it that St George got eighteen before lunch, but that was making too much of a good thing. There is a very interesting photograph in the book of an angler playing a salmon from a boat in saltwater. This is thought to be in the area of what are now called the Road Pools.

The register gives details of incredible fishing experienced by St George after he left Screebe in 1913. In 1914, between 13 June and 4 July he took 175 salmon averaging 20.27 pounds from the Moisie river in Canada. His party had 265 fish from the Bellingham beat of the Wye in 1916, averaging 16.87 pounds. St George fished Delfour on the Spey, and Upper Floors and Sprouston on the Tweed in 1917; on 17 November he landed Tweed fish of 33, 23, 23, 20 and 12 pounds. On 16 February 1921, he had seven Tweed fish, six between seven and a half and nine and a half pounds, and one weighing 51 pounds. The big fish was hooked and landed at dusk, and although the register is not entirely clear, it seems to have taken a fly dressed on a 2/0 hook fished on a fourteen foot rod. (By a coincidence, just after I first fished Screebe I bought a second-hand copy of one of my favourite fishing books, A. H. Chaytor's *Letters to a Salmon Fisher's Sons,* the second printing of 1910. There is a dedication on the fly-leaf, in good Victorian copperplate script, matching the hand which inscribed details of those mighty fish in the register, 'To W. H. Cooper from H. St George').

Nowadays, anglers are travelling in the opposite direction, and Screebe sees many continental parties fishing in the summer months. A former world casting champion and world record holder, in the single-handed fly event, Hans Ruedi Hebeisen from Zürich, brings parties of Swiss and German anglers to the fishery and many of them go home with their first salmon. However there is certainly room for more fishing effort, and the current annual average of between one hundred and two hundred fish does not reflect the potential of the system. During a recent stay, both Bob Hutchinson and myself hooked fish on my first morning, before we were becalmed under hot sunshine. The next day a boat rose and missed two fish, and one was taken from one of the piers on Screebe Lough. The following morning, I had a fish before breakfast, Hans Ruedi took another just after breakfast, and a Swiss angler lost a good fish after a long fight. I had to leave at lunch-time, so I did not see what happened in the afternoon, but I would have been surprised if at least a couple of salmon were not added to the bag. I saw fish, in numbers, throughout the system. A couple of weeks later, Bob and his son had seven fish in a day.

Like many salmon anglers, I 'collect' salmon, and I hope eventually to have taken fish, perhaps only one fish, from each of the major Irish salmon fisheries. All salmon are remarkable, but a Screebe salmon, from a fishery in that landscape and with such a history, is a special fish.

CHAPTER 8

The Salmon Rivers of the Foyle System

Junction pools make great salmon beats the world over. On the Foyle system, the confluence of the River Derg with the River Mourne is known as the Snaa water, and is one of the choice streams on the whole of this great network of salmon rivers. It is part of the Abercorn Estate fishery. The Mourne is a big river here, over fifty yards wide, rushing from rough streams to glides over boulders and rock ledges. A few hundred yards below the Snaa water is a stretch called Feddens. The left bank is very steep, thickly covered by broad-leaved trees, and falls to a jumble of rocks by the water side; it is very rough going.

As you travel from salmon river to salmon river in Ireland, one of the variations you first notice is casting style. It is curious how little it has been remarked upon. Of course we all know about the Spey cast, but this has become part of a limited formal repertoire of technique, and not recognised for what it really is – one of the many local adaptations in style required by the run of a river and the lie of its banks.

As you try to perch on a rock or a grassy incline by the left side of Feddens, you wonder how you will deliver a fly, on a sufficient length of line, in these fast streams. The Spey cast is the obvious answer, but not the whole one. On this side of the river, the rock ledges begin to show when the gauge on the far bank is at or below the two inch mark, a good fishing height. These ledges snag any low moving fly, and litter the splash-down zone for the single Spey cast. I pondered all this the first time I fished the beat, in the company of one of the local rods, Frank Elliott of Strabane. Frank is a discriminating angler, with a precise mind, and a memory like a steel trap for the events of his long association with the Mourne. He has been fishing the river for fifty years.

Now a first stage in the salmon angler's education is the realisation of the importance of The Knowledge. This is knowing where fish lie and where they can be taken, at all the water heights, and conditions of colour and temperature which the angler will meet on a beat throughout the year. It takes a long time to accumulate, but as it accrues, the angler's technique develops correspondingly. As he discovers the lies he also learns the practicable ways to address them. Here is the core of the fly-fisher's craft. The length of line, the angle of the cast, the speed of swing are probably more critical in salmon fly-fishing than in any other type of angling, and are the reasons why, on any river, a small group of skilful anglers consistently record heavier bags than the other rods.

With this in mind, I was very attentive to what Frank was doing when I fished with him on the Mourne that day. Clearly everything depended on the cast, especially since he wore only thigh boots, and could not gain advantages of angle and length from deep wading. He used a fifteen foot rod, like all the Mourne regulars whom I met, with a number eleven line. His standard length of cast was about twenty-five yards. He lifted off for the back cast in a conventional way, but instead of bringing the line straight back above his right shoulder, he angled it around behind him, opposite the direction of the forward thrust, and contrived a very low trajectory. The line punched back and straightened out at hip height, and then was shot forward, high, in a narrow loop which unrolled perfectly from rod tip to fly. It is a kind of switch cast. The precision of the back cast was remarkable. If it had been lifted high, in regulation form, it would have caught the trees on the high bank. It seemed to fly into the gap between tree line and grass with practised consistency, and I did not see him get hung up at any time. According to Frank, a priest once explained the difference between the salmon casts which involve a change of direction in this way: if the fly touches water on the back cast it is a Spey cast; if it doesn't, it is a switch cast; and if it goes where you intend, it is a miracle.

Anglers on the opposite, right, bank have different problems, and have adapted in their own way. The following day I saw this in the style of Davy Campbell of Newtownstewart, who although normally right-handed, casts left-handed here. He also fished almost the whole line, with a fifteen foot rod, unfurling a tight loop of line into popply water on the far side, so as to let it swing steadily across a big V of gliding current which arrowed into a rough run over small rocks – easily recognisable as one of the main taking zones on the stretch. The general standard of fly casting on this difficult beat was very high, and the length of line fished was the longest I have seen in Ireland.

The Mourne may be the only river in Ireland where a big rod and heavy line are part of the regular armoury for July; it was the second of the month when I fished with Frank, and the size of the flies corresponded to the long rods in use. We were fishing for grilse, the first wave of the main run had just crossed the weir at Sion Mills on big water and were making for the Derg, yet we were using flies dressed on size six or eight trebles. Sandy Vance had five fish on a size four single that day. These are massive hooks in comparison to those used on any of the western seaboard rivers, with the possible exception of the Shannon, for grilse at this time of year, but everything about the Mourne is on a generous scale, including the welcome given to a stranger that day by a most friendly company of anglers.

*   *   *

Although its rivers are individually distinctive, the Foyle system, for the purposes of its salmon fishing, is primarily a family of waters, and ranks with the Moy

Opposite: The Falls Pool, River Finn.

system as perhaps the premier salmon fishery in Ireland. It comprises the Foyle itself, which is formed by the confluence of the Finn and the Mourne at Lifford Bridge; the Finn, which flows from Donegal and whose lower course, from Clady, charts the border between the Republic and Northern Ireland; the Mourne, which local anglers regard as that stretch of river between Newtownstewart and Lifford Bridge; the Derg, which issues from Lough Derg in the Republic and joins the Mourne at the Snaa water; the Strule, which is the name of the river upstream of Newtownstewart. And these are just the main watercourses, given their commonly-used names. There are other local names for the same streams, and there are many important additional tributaries, such as the Owenkillew and the Gleneally rivers. The names alone are enough to make the head spin, but the rivers are also distinguished by the pattern of their salmon runs, and by their misbehaviour after rain.

The total run of salmon into this system is huge. In one recent year the drift nets had 80,000 fish; in a normal year the total might be 30,000 – 40,000. It is an enormously important sporting resource for communities on both sides of the border. Indeed this was recognised, despite tensions in the political background, in the early 1950s. Two Canadian consultants, Elson and Toumi were engaged to investigate and report on the fishery. They recommended a unitary management regime for the system, and restraints on commercial netting. So the Foyle Fisheries Commission was set up, in 1952, by the concerted action of the Irish and Northern Irish governments, to manage the whole system regardless of national boundaries. One of the principal recommendations of the consultants was to put back the opening date for netting, initially for a five year period. The nets would not be allowed to start until the third Monday in June. This regime continued for twelve rather than five years, and now the nets come on around the 16 June, and must finish by the end of July. There is a seventy-two hour slap at weekends, and a further limitation is enforced if less than 2,000 fish are registered on the counter at Sion Mills weir, and the gauge shows at least twenty-two inches of water. When this occurs, netting is restricted for an extra forty-eight hours.

The consultants had been called in because of a decline in stocks, especially in the run of big grilse, six to eight pound fish which used to run the Mourne but which have not been seen now for some years. What has been gained is a huge increase in the early grilse run of late May and the beginning of June, and a steady recovery of the later runs once imperilled by the netsmen.

The system has a spring run, over sixty per cent of which is composed of River Finn fish. These come in during the last week of March and the first weeks of April. Although the Finn gets the bulk of the run, the Mourne below Sion Mills has been recording a steady increase in the take.

The grilse run begins in late May and early June and is again composed mainly of River Finn fish. These run right up the river, to the Cloghan Lodge water, and are held up by the Falls there until late June. Some of these grilse also run the Mourne, usually stopping at the Sion Mills weir unless the water is high, when they push on and turn into the Derg. Almost all the early Mourne grilse run into the Derg, which has good spawning sites. A July run of grilse augments the early runs on the Derg, and also populates the Strule. Some big summer fish run with these grilse. At this time of year sea-trout also appear in numbers, and head for the Gleneally. This river, and the Owenkillew are run by only a few salmon before August and September. The late fish can appear in numbers and run all the rivers of the system. Like late salmon everywhere, although they are fresh, they have often coloured up in the estuary, and show russet sides as they leap on their way up the rivers. A strain of big fish, known locally as the Black School, sometimes show in September

For the angler it is important to know that the behaviour of the rivers is as variable as the behaviour of its salmon. The Finn and the Derg watersheds lie in the mountains of Donegal, whereas the Strule and its tributaries are fed from the Sperrins in the east and a range of hills to the south. The same weather systems may load the different watersheds at different rates, and even locals find it almost impossible to predict, from actual rainfall, let alone weather forecasts, how the rivers will behave.

Here is an example: I was on the Mourne at the New Bridge, where the Derg flows in, on a morning in early July. A low pressure system had passed over during the night, with heavy rain, and we waited for the rivers to rise. The Mourne did rise a few inches, and coloured a little, but was fishable. The Derg showed some of the Derg weed, soft bottom weed torn away by rising water and a sure harbinger of a flood. It was also rising and colouring, but slowly, so it seemed there might be fishing on the river, which can fall quickly, after lunch. When I returned, the water was beginning to drop and the white water was now actually white rather than sepia. I delayed for a few hours before driving upstream to Ardstraw, where there are five miles of lovely streams. I made my way across small meadows with lines of cut hay lying frail under the high-built clouds of midsummer. You hear a brimming river before you see it, but still I could hardly believe the sight of the glossy brown stream, batting the low boughs of bankside trees, swirling in deep eddies and bearing knots of bright green weed. The river had risen, not by inches but by feet, since I had last seen it, and was unfishable. We did not see the rain in Donegal which had been responsible for this. I turned back to Ardstraw where a couple of men with rods and nets leaned over the narrow stone bridge, watching for any sign of a fall. I had heard that the Derg fell quickly, but they thought, rightly, that there would not be any more fishing that day.

Another example: Davy Campbell knocked at my door at half past five in the morning, but I had already been wakened by drumming rain on the roof. The previous day on the Mourne had been a good one and Davy hoped to get a few hours fishing before going to work in his fishing tackle shop, especially as it seemed that the rain would put several inches on the river and render it useless for the fly for some time. The Mourne is slow to rise and holds steady for some time, so that one good flood can give a week or more of fishing, but we were still surprised to see the gauge by the hut at two inches, the same level as the previous day, and the river show clear with no weed. The water was good and the air was fresh, so I came back an hour after breakfast to resume. I had risen two fish in the earlier session, grilse showed steadily, and the day was set fair for good sport. Twice I waded down a length of river where grilse lay, without stirring anything; after the first time I noticed weed float by, and motes of suspended matter seemed to thicken the water. The gauge still showed two inches. But after the second run down the gauge showed three inches, and then twenty minutes later four inches. I

91

reeled up. The river had risen, though not with the rain we had experienced but rather with heavier and later falls in the eastern watershed which had taken some hours to work through. Fishing for the day was finished.

*   *   *

The quality of salmon fishing on the Foyle system has been obscured by waves of political disturbance which have rolled over this part of the island for almost all of this century. Yet the fishing has always been good; so good that in the early 1900s the Abercorn Hotel at Newtownstewart was filled with fishermen for the best weeks of the season. The records of T.P. Dobson illustrate the quality of sport which brought them up. He fished the river, and its tributaries in the area of Newtownstewart from 1906 to 1945. In that time he caught 2,910 salmon from the river. Between 1906 and 1927 he caught 1,818 of these fish. His best year was 1922, when he had 234. He took 110 in 1908, 124 in 1909, 75 in 1911 (he had 8 in one day in this year), 122 in 1912, 155 in 1913. He had good numbers of fish between ten and twenty pounds, so this is by no means a record of small grilse catches.

Anglers still catch numbers of salmon from the system which would be remarkable elsewhere. Ted Browne, the doyen of anglers on the Feddens stretch averages sixty to seventy fish a year from that water and the Finn. Frank Elliott has taken over 1,400 salmon in a lifetime of fishing the Foyle system. He caught his first on 12 July 1948 when he was ten years old. He has killed spring fish in every March since 1952, except for one year when he hooked five and lost them all. His biggest weighed nineteen pounds. His best run was in the early 1980s when he had eleven springers from 5–12 April.

Jack Russell, manager of Russell's Bakeries where Frank worked in the early 1950s, was a man of fixed habits. He headed for work in his Jaguar, one of the few in Northern Ireland in those days, crossing Lifford Bridge at about the same time, a quarter past ten, every day. On the 14, 15, 16 March in one particular year, he saw Frank playing salmon on each of those consecutive days, at the same time, and each time pulled in to see the fish landed.

Lifford Bridge is quite a wide span sheltering known salmon lies. Sean McLoughlin, County Manager of Donegal, had one of the most celebrated captures when fishing from this bridge. He hooked and landed a salmon on a Devon Minnow inadvertently placed tail up on the trace. The fish did not mind and Sean became famous for it.

The water just upstream of Lifford Bridge, to the confluence of the Mourne and the Finn, is still free fishing. It is also excellent fishing when the rivers are low and the fish back up here, waiting for the stimulus of a flood. Downstream the fishing is also good, especially for sea-trout, for a distance of a mile or so. There is now a nominal charge to fish here. Frank has fished the river around the bridge since childhood, as it is only a short way from his home in Strabane. He was once asked by a visitor which were the good flies for sea-trout here and he gave a list, including a fly called Jacob's Ladder. The following year the same thing happened, but the visitor said that he had had difficulty finding a source for the fly. Frank mentioned that Rogan of Ballyshannon might be able to provide copies

A spring salmon from the Graveyard Pool, River Finn.

of the dressing. Some time afterwards he received a package containing the flies and some other material, with a letter of thanks from Kingsmill-Moore, who had been the summer visitor.

*   *   *

There is great variation in the character, and the styles of fishing, of each of the rivers of the Foyle system. In July I fished for grilse on the Mourne with a fifteen foot rod, a heavy line and big flies, tackle normally associated with spring fish. Two months earlier I had fished the Finn for spring salmon with single-handed and short double-handed rods and number seven and eight lines.

The Finn has all the attributes of a classic spate river, although it is much more substantial than most, and in its lower course a levelling gradient and deeper runs give it a steadier character than the swift and skittish river above Cloghan Lodge. It can be as much as fifty yards wide in the middle reaches, but even so the water foams over rough bedrock and boulders. Stand at the Ivy bridge just below Cloghan Lodge and look downstream; you will see a river gushing from pool to pool, some not bigger than a dining table, each formed by natural croys of rock projecting from either bank. In late May or early June you will also see the small spurts as grilse run into each pool. The last time I stood on the bridge I saw exactly this; and a moment later I watched an angler bending into the fish which had just run in, because it had almost immediately taken his lure.

I first fished the Finn in the company of Tommy Simpson on a day in late May when the river was running down after a flood and a particularly good mix of late spring fish and grilse were in. We went first to a pool several hundred yards long, closely bordered by trees and low banks on either side. The river bed smoothed out at this point, from a rubble of big rocks which formed shallow runs upstream, to a deeper and smoother run, which nevertheless concealed enough stones to trip the unwary wader. Like any of the Finn pools I have fished, this had a definite wading line which had to be followed if one were to remain dry. It was identified by a spine of current, sharp and rough at first as it ran through the median line of the river, then less distinct when it veered toward the right bank and turned back toward the left bank. The fainter the sign the more important it was to discern it, because by then the water was up to my waist and pushing me steadily forward. Water height has to be judged very carefully; from about mid-way on this pool there is no way to go but forward, and the quality of your judgement will determine whether you wade or swim.

The fish lay mostly in deep water under the right bank. I saw a bait fisher land a silver springer of over ten pounds, then Tommy, coming down behind me, hooked and landed a grilse of about four pounds. Shortly after, a third angler who followed us down landed a thirteen pound springer, fresh in. The two fish which took fly both fell to shrimp patterns, which are *de rigeur* in this part of the world. The bigger fish took a size twelve Curry's Red Shrimp, now a standard fly for these rivers. Tommy had his fish on a fly of his own devising, a shrimp pattern of course. Most fly anglers use long single-handed rods on this fishery; I started with my standard spate river outfit for western rivers, a nine foot rod and a WF7F line. This is fine for casting on slow pools but the line profile was inadequate for streamy water, where switch casting was required. In addition, the Finn flows north-west/south-east, and there is often a following wind, which blows onto the right shoulder of anglers fishing from the left side of the river as we were. I found the fishing much easier when I changed to a thirteen foot rod, a number eight double tapered line, and a Spey casting style to deliver the flies.

A curiosity of this fishing is that anglers who are habitués, like Tommy, let the fly fish very slowly indeed in slack water, without any hand-lining, and take plenty of salmon. I had to restrain myself from pulling the flies. Grilse and springers lie in both types of water at this time of year. Tommy took an eleven pound springer later that day from the narrow throat of a pool and played it out in water only a couple of feet deep. Its runs upstream raised an audible hiss as the line cut through rough stickles.

This stretch of the river may be fished by either fly or bait, which is perhaps too great a concession to the latter as so much of it is perfect fly water. There are enough rivers for the wormers and the spinners; such fine streams should be preserved for the best sport that can be had with rod and line – the pursuit of the salmon with the fly. And the Finn has miles of such water; it is undoubtedly one of the best salmon fisheries in Ireland. The steep gradient of the river and the very rocky bottom allow fish to lie, and the fly-fisher to address them in lively water even at relatively low levels. For example, there is a very good pool on the Cloghan water called Keys Pool, which has a rough sharp running in at the head, and then a fast stream which turns into a smooth run plaited with purls of current under the trees of the left bank. One fishes it from a nice gravel slope on the right bank. In all but very high water this holds lots of fish, though it can be a little slow when the levels fall. When they drop too low all you do is head upstream, where there are miles of very rough river bed; the streams spill between boulders, holding grilse when they are running, at all heights, and providing enough life to work the fly nicely. Some of these streams have to be waded deep, and you need steel tackets or felt on the soles of your boots to get a purchase. The ground is very uneven; there are depressions around the biggest rocks deep enough to give you a surprise.

There is one part of this reach of the Finn which is really only fishable with bait. This is the stretch of river at the Falls, known as the Sanctuary. Steep rock faces form a gorge here, and the river churns through narrow passes in a froth of white water with the amber tints. Anglers, usually fishing worm, perch on rock ledges ten or fifteen feet above the river; when they hook fish they lead them into little quiet bays and then heave them out by main force. Playing and landing are conventional terms that do not apply to the fishing in the Sanctuary. The Falls are a natural barrier above which few fish move until about mid-June. Then grilse run way upriver, to the headwaters of the Reelan tributary, and as far as Lough Finn at the top of the watershed.

*   *   *

Fishing tackle shops are as much about the exchange of gossip, and the latest intelligence on local fishing, as about retail selling. Davy Campbell's shop in Newtownstewart is the nerve centre of local angling intelligence.

Newtownstewart is well-placed; a great ox-bow of the Mourne surrounds the town, and a big tributary enters the main river here. The Derg flows into the main river just down the road. On any morning when the fish are running, local anglers will drop in, or phone, to find out about the state of the rivers and the previous day's catches. Much of the information is provided by Davy himself, from his experiences on his beats of the Mourne or its tributaries.

His house is on the right side of the Owenkillew valley, separated by a road and a narrow field from the river. We strolled down to it one evening, after putting our rods up on his front lawn, and as we walked just a hundred yards over a stubbled field to the bankside, I thought that he was a fortunate man. The terrain here is quite unlike the mountainous hinterland of the upper Finn. It is a rolling landscape of small hills, neat fields, and well-ordered farmyards, with the intimacy of scale peculiar to drumlin country. Each small house seems to have its own beehives. The country roads, uniquely, are named with road signs such as one would usually find in towns.

The Mourne and its tributaries have an extraordinary velocity for such a lowland setting. The Owenkillew may twist and turn over the apparently gentle landscape, but it is as swift and spatey as its brethren. It has cut a wide channel, most of it exposed gravels and stones when the water is low. But even then the shrunken stream is quick and deep enough to make the line thrum as it sweeps the surface. The wading is easier, certainly than on the Mourne, and the fishing daintier. A long single-handed rod, of perhaps ten feet, with a double tapered line will command all the fishable water.

That evening we went down on the off-chance that a grilse or two might have made its way up, in advance of the main run in August. I first fished a far bank run, where trees bowed over the quick streams, split by projecting boulders. We then forded the river and walked the left bank, through a farmyard, to a bend where the stream ran in a tight curve against the far bank, and the fly fished beautifully all the way down; this run turns into a glide just around the corner, which then breaks over stones into a rough stream. As Davy joined me he mentioned that the very point of the V of the glide was, as I had guessed, a good taking spot, and he confirmed this by clipping his fly into it and rising a fish, which took on the next presentation; it was an early sea-trout. This stream, and the deep pool below, are prime sea-trout water in late July and August, and some of the best sea-trout fishing on the whole system is to be had on pools like these in the Gleneally and the Owenkillew. We continued down the river, turning out into the road and then cutting in again through the small sloping and shaved fields in the dusk, still but for the white scuts of rabbits hopping across them. We met the river again at the bottom of the deep pool, which we were just able to cross at the point where it spilled into a rapid over big rocks. There is no group of rivers in any part of Ireland which needs wading skills like those of the Foyle system.

The Foyle is a great system with unique contrasts of landscape and habitat. That so few people outside its immediate hinterland should know it is understandable given the turbulence in Northern Ireland in the last twenty-five years, but it is as much their loss, as it is a loss to the good anglers of those lovely rivers.

CHAPTER 9

The Evening Rise

In mid-July the evenings are so long that I can afford to have dinner quickly, as soon as I return from work, before gathering tackle and setting out for the river, about an hour's drive away. The hedgerows on roads in this part of Ireland are lush. They close in as soon as I turn off onto a minor road which twists from one blind bend to another. I drive slowly; there's often a tractor with a load of hay; or a herd of cattle, around the corner. The road winds up and down low hills, and the sound of the engine bounces directly back from dense foliage through the open windows. I bump up the rutted lane and the medieval ruin comes into view. No cars are here so I will be on my own for a while. Quite often I have the place to myself for the whole evening, that is about a mile of water, double bank. Mind you, it is not surprising because this can be really difficult fishing.

I make my way over the old bridge, one of the many handsome and solid spans which adorn this historic valley. Wherever you are on the Boyne there always

Fishing the evening rise, River Boyne.

seems to be a relic of earlier settlement overlooking you. There are the great bronze age tumuli of Knowth, Newgrange and Dowth, passage-grave sites of European importance. The ruined fortifications on the bank at Trim mark the largest Anglo-Norman castle built in Ireland, and all along the river are well-maintained Georgian and Victorian mansions. Of course the Boyne also gave its name to the battle, fought in July 1690, in the area now called Oldbridge, though this was a mere episode in the long historic associations of this great Irish river.

This upper water looks very nice, deep and glidey, but I have never done well there. The lads at the farmhouse get good fish from it early in the season, one or two of them over four pounds, on the wet fly. I follow my usual routine and go down past the weir where there is about a quarter of a mile of shallow water here which is just right for the first stage of the evening rise, when the smaller fish start getting at the duns and spinners which begin to come down. Not just small fish either, if, as usually happens at this time of year, the blue winged olive appears. The banks are good but the stream is full of weed, even though this is a big river, more than thirty yards wide here. So I use chest waders for this part of the evening. You have to get in carefully because the ground nearest the bank is often sucky mud. A little farther out the going gets better, and you feel the hard marl under your feet. The limestone here is firm and takes your weight without absorbing it – on some limestone loughs the marl is dangerous stuff; you can sink into it up to your oxters. However, care is still needed because the bed is very lumpy, and you can take a spill if you aren't watchful.

Once in the river you can address fish lying in the channels which are formed by the thick beds of weed. And, what is more important at this time of evening, you can see more clearly what they are taking. Trout here will take a hatching nymph, a dun or a spinner, and then slash at a sedge in as many minutes. This is not indiscriminate feeding however, as you find when you put your artificial over that fish for the fiftieth time without a hint of weakening on its part.

It is still quite early, so I wait until the fly come up in earnest and the fish show. There are fly about: in the stillness you can hear the swallows' beaks snap on them. Some birds skim so low that they leave a trail in the surface. Last year I was watching them like this when a sparrowhawk came from nowhere and took one on the wing. He flew with it to the field opposite, but was so mobbed by the rest of the flight that he allowed it to escape.

The water is quite low, which makes for easy wading. I would prefer a slight rise in levels, the kind you get after rain which isn't enough to inject a strong colour into the river, but is sufficient to raise it a few inches. For some reason this prompts the fly to appear quite early, and the trout to rise more freely, and rather earlier, than they would usually do. The first fly to appear this evening are, as usual, the smaller species. A few fish begin to show to these but they are extremely picky and for the most part just oncers, so unless I see one of these show a bit of consistency, I ignore them. I have a four pound test leader attached for this part of the evening rise, and a selection of Blue Winged Olive (BWO) imitations. I know where a couple of good fish live, so I rove quietly up and down the bank looking for one of these fish to show, and I am pretty sure that they will only get in the mood if there is a hatch of blue winged olives.

Now some blue winged olives are beginning to appear, so I keep a sharp eye on my candidates, and sure enough as I approach one he is up in the water. I get well below him, and wade quietly into position. The geography of this river, with its wide shallow bed and the banks of weed creating narrow runs, helps to conceal my approach, and I can get into range so as to have a good shot. I am about fifteen yards below the fish, which is lying slightly to my left. He is in a channel some five feet wide, and in only three or four feet of water. A good scatter of blue winged olives are coming down, and the fish is really on. It fields the fly with a will, rolling this way and that, and even at rest its dorsal and tail fins are out of the water. The trick is to see what phase of the fly it is taking. On the Boyne, in my experience, at this stage of the rise, the nymph is on the menu, and that's certainly what's happening here, although this fish is also taking the occasional winged fly. There are no spinner yet. Now here's a situation which can drive anyone straight home. I am within fifteen yards of a good fish, certainly over three pounds. It is feeding hard, and I am pretty sure what species it is taking. After half an hour, it has not been scared it but it has not risen either, although I have sent artificial after artificial fly over it. I give it best and move on to another trout.

Here is one in a similar holt, but clearly a smaller fish, and as I get in and below him I also see that he's not fixed on the nymph, but is taking a lot of winged fly. I put up a size fifteen Pheasant Tail and get it to him nicely and he takes it well. He leaps on feeling the hook, then runs around, but does not go to weed so I can work him back to me and into the net. A nice fish of a pound, and quite silvery.

There are more sedge about and it is almost nine o' clock, so time to prepare for sedge fishing. But there is one last chance of picking up a fish on the small fly, so I make my way to a big pool, where the river spreads after running fast and straight, and makes a large eddy on my side. I have not caught one of the really big Boyne fish but I have seen several, and one lives, out of reach, on the far side of this pool. I saw him come up once, and that huge side flashing bronze just under the surface was really something; the fish must be eight pounds or more. A trout of that size was caught a few hundred yards downstream last season, on a dry sedge. As I thought, there are fish rising steadily just on the edge of the stream, but at this stage of the rise it is almost impossible to make out what they are taking. The rises are dainty, quite unlike the vigorous swirls to blue winged olive nymph which that big fish was making earlier and, as there are relatively few duns about, I put on a spinner. I choose a size eighteen fly, with a pale body and synthetic wings, white, tied flat. The cast is short, and I aim high and stop the forward stroke sharply, to recoil the leader. The fly drops softly, with slack behind it, so it gets a good float. I do this perhaps fifteen times before I get a sipping take and pull tight to the fish. It runs off against the reel, but the hook slips free.

Now for the sedge. This is always a difficult choice because fish will go on taking BWO right into darkness, but I will need to change to stronger nylon soon, as I do not like using less than six pound material in this weedy water, with big fish about, in poor light. And if I go up to six pound test, I will no longer be fishing small flies. I put up a size twelve sedge, with a deer-hair wing for added buoyancy.

Trout are already beginning to take sedge with the aptly termed slashing rise, but I never do well with the fly on this river until the light is quite thick, and I have caught a number of fish in utter darkness. It is not uncommon to get them up to midnight in the really long evenings of late June and July when sedge fishing on the river is at its best.

You need to have both the rod and the rhythm for this work, because in most sedge fishing you are casting blind at the sound of a rise. I have a very nice nine footer, an American rod with a parabolic action; one can almost feel the click as the back and forward strokes travel down the tapers well into the middle section; this is needed as there is hardly more tactile fishing than casting a dry fly, in the dark, to rises you cannot see.

I have not moved position but I am now targeting rising fish in the fast run into the eddy. There is one in a good position, on my side of the river, about fifteen yards away, and coming up regularly. I lengthen line, not straining but letting my arm follow the rhythm of the rod. Luckily there's little wind; wind at dusk can kill the fly, but, more importantly, it destroys the sense of feel that is your only link with the trout out there. The line is flowing out nicely, and I put down the fly and let it drift, and I do this and pick it off, twice, before there is a swish in the darkness where my fly should be, and I strike into the fish. He runs all over the place, I have no idea where at first, until I get him under control and he bores around under my feet. I can just see enough to get the net under him, another good fish of a pound and a half. I could stay a bit longer, but I have to work tomorrow, and I still have the drive home. It's eleven o' clock. I'm guided up the hill and through the pasture by the farm lights. I can hear two women at the door saying their farewells with a clarity that would unnerve them. The dogs create hell as I go past, but they will not mind me for long because soon I'm in the car, driving along the tunnel of the headlights through absolute blackness, and looking forward to a cup of tea in a sleeping house.

* * *

The Boyne has always been a river for big fish, both trout and salmon. The spring salmon were magnificent, and averaged in the high teens of pounds. Jim Reynolds' book *A Life by the Boyne* (privately published under Zircon Press imprint in 1989) has grainy black and white pictures of some of these giants, of up to 35 pounds. Reynolds also publishes figures for the Mollies fishery, supplied by Chris Pringle, a former member of the Mollies syndicate. The Mollies (from the Irish malaí, meaning brow) is the first fishery on the Meath Blackwater, upstream from its confluence with the Boyne, in Navan town. These days it is run down, and the old snags have been supplemented by supermarket trolleys and other urban detritus, but back in the 1950s and 1960s a rod on the Mollies was something to die for. This seems hardly credible for a water that has all the character of an industrial canal, and a 'beat' gave you less room than a Lancashire roach fisher would have enjoyed in a works match. The fishery was 180 yards long with an average width of nine yards. A.A. Luce reckoned that in high water it could comfortably accommodate six rods, three on either side. In 1965 the Mollies produced 105 fish, and in 1966, the *annus mirabilis*, 187 fish. Returns fell off severely from 1970. But remember those fish were all big Boyne springers. We can hardly imagine, in these times when a springer averages about nine pounds, what hooking and holding one of these submarines was like, but I know of two people who have first-hand experience. In 1966 Frank Luce landed a thirty-eight pound fish from that two hundred yard by nine yard stretch of water, and within two weeks of Luce getting his fish, Rory Harkin also took a big one.

Rory fished the Stackallen water, some miles downstream of Navan. This is a very wide section of river, and fishable even in very heavy water. On that February day, Rory got to the river and fished through a biting cold wind, which crisped the snow lying on the fields. He had arrived early, and mid-morning he went back to his car to get a cup of tea. The fishing seemed poor, and the air so cold, that he didn't feel optimistic. He had left his rod at the riverbank, and but for that he would have been on his way back to Dublin when he had emptied his flask. So he went back to the river to collect his rod and, having a last cast, threw from one of the barges moored by the bank at that point. His Oxblood and Gold Devon landed in mid-river, falling short; he began to retrieve, and was at once into a fish. It stayed down, but yielded surprisingly quickly, and within two minutes he had it ready for landing. It must just have settled in a lie, having run quick and far (it was sea-liced), because it weighed thirty-three pounds, and a Boyne fish of that size usually took a long time to subdue. In fact, that afternoon he hooked a seventeen pounder which took over a quarter of an hour to master.

Sedge time on the Liffey.

That made a brace for the day *averaging* twenty-five pounds each.

Although 1966 was the last really good year for Boyne springers, the river has been a noted salmon river for over a century. Grimble (*The Salmon Rivers of Ireland*) dwells lovingly on the Boyne which was obviously an esteemed river when he wrote in 1913, 'Salmon run heavy, and the first fifty that are got on the Black Castle waters [just below Navan] will sometimes show the remarkable average of 20 lbs . . . for as these first fifty will all be got by the end of March, it will be seen that such a catch will take some beating; while for weight, irrespective of numbers, there is hardly a river in the United Kingdom that can equal it.'

Numbers also were high in some years, and 1966 was not a patch on 1885, when 794 fish were taken on the Black Castle waters, and 56 were killed in a day by four rods; 199 in eight days. '. . . we do not think that this total of 56 *spring* fish, taken in one day, by the four rods of Messrs Fitzherbert, from two miles of river, has ever been beaten in the United Kingdom'.

The spring fish have now almost completely gone, though there are signs of hope from time to time. As I write, in April 1996, I have just learned that sixteen fish were caught from the river at Navan over a recent weekend. There was a brief revival in the mid-1980s, and some big fish were got, particularly in the areas of the Ramparts, and the Mollies, in Navan. I fished there a little at this time and one March evening on the Upper Black Castle, I saw a figure approach on the far bank, carrying a salmon, which even at a distance I knew to be a good fish. It was Frank Luce carrying a seventeen pounder, a perfectly shaped Boyne springer.

Sometimes a run of smaller fish appears around late April, but you would not want to depend on it. A sizeable run of summer fish does come in during July and August, but these are sometimes confined to the lower reaches and are mostly taken by bait, many of them in Curly Hole near Oldbridge. This place heaves with fish in a dry summer, but they are often stale by then.

Despite the barbarous work by the dredgers, begun in 1969, which has changed the river irrevocably, the Boyne remains a great river. It has a series of very good clubs, well served by officers like the late Stephen Monaghan of the Navan Anglers Association, or Charlie Woods of the Bective Club. The fly have re-established themselves; there is even a good mayfly hatch. We can lament, with Jim Reynolds, the loss of the majestic natural watercourse, and the fishing of the 1950s and 1960s, but we can also enjoy what is left to us.

*   *   *

The evening rise is fished all over Ireland on rivers large and small. The Boyne fishing is specialised by national standards; the fish are big and difficult, and on some evenings you have the weary feeling, when setting out, of going for another hiding from a very difficult adversary.

I have had cheerful sport with small brown trout in a number of rivers, such as the Robe near Ballinrobe, or the Suir in its middle reaches, when you knew that if the fly were up then you would get a fish or two. The Robe fish announced themselves with generous rises, then when you put a fly to them it drifted slowly on the flat surface before a fish would boil and be hooked. The trout of the middle Suir were also ready risers, and I have had evenings on the river upstream of Clonmel when the fly would produce half a dozen fish to a pound weight.

However, that stretch of the Suir was not typical of the river as a whole. It had a shifting bed of loose gravel and the trout were numerous and willing. Go downstream to the heavy flows over a limestone bed and you find the epicures which can be really difficult to tempt with a fly on a summer's evening. I would say that as a whole, evening fishing on a limestone river is relatively difficult fishing, hard to master but with great rewards. My defining experience of the evening rise on a limestone river came on the Fergus, in County Clare, on a September evening. I was on a lovely stretch of the river, a few miles above Lough Inchiquin. A smooth pasture bounded my right bank; the river flowed full, with a surface like satin in the evening light. I had a selection of dry flies, proven elsewhere, and waited my chance. The rise started quite smartly, and soon fish were showing all over the river. They were taking BWO. I covered one after another, with all the flies in my box, and covered them delicately and well; but I got no more than a few short takes in two hours of extreme frustration. This experience is not untypical. You often come away feeling that you ought to have done better. And you rarely have, in any other dry-fly fishing, as many refusals as you have during the evening rise.

I first came across this selectivity, and experienced the vagaries of the evening rise, on the Liffey, the rich lower stretches around Clane, where trout average a pound in weight and grow to five or six pounds. The river is stocked here, but there are also good wild fish. Some evenings were just long sequences of frustration, compounded by having to climb barbed wire fences every hundred yards. You might wander a quarter of a mile in the early evening looking for a steady rising trout but finding only oncers in the familiar places. I put many a fly to these but rarely brought one up. As the evening waned a harsh wind might come up or a persistent rain set in and then you might as well go home. On some of these evenings you hardly cast a fly.

I learned early that it was essential to know the lie of the river, where the fish were, and where the fly were. The difference was that some short lengths were always good for quality trout and, if you took one or two out of it in an evening, within a few days' time others would have taken their place. There was an excellent stretch, ideal for fly-fishing, where streamer weed grew on the shallow gravels on my bank, and I could wade into this and fish very precisely to trout rising in a channel only six feet wide, where the river was pinched in between the weed and the bank. There were lovely trout here and I had some nice ones from it. I got one on a windy evening in late summer, when I made my way here towards dusk. Windy evenings are generally not good, but this evening there was a fish rising in a little bay in the far bank, in a tiny eddy out of the main current. It was a shot that needed nice judgement, but this once I got it right and my fly floated over on the following wind and lighted in the bay just a foot above the fish. He had it with a wallop and then motored upstream, deep and strong. All the frustrations of other evenings sharpened the thrill of that moment.

That was a place where the fish, the good fish, were. But other reaches used to produce great hatches of a little silver sedge, specially prolific on this part of the Liffey. The fly came out at dusk, and in the half light the river became alive with fish rising to a blizzard of sedge. The fish were mainly small, but there were so many, and the fly so thick, that the usual rules of the evening rise, looking for and addressing a specific feeding fish, had to be forgotten. The best way of attacking these trout was to put up a buoyant sedge, douse it with floatant, and then cast it across and let the current swing it in a skidding traverse across the river. Trout went mad for it and you might hook every fifth or more take.

*   *   *

No matter how frustrating, the evening rise will always be tinged with a little hope, because on waters with big wild brown trout it is one of the few times when they are takeable. In fact there are really only two occasions: one is with the sedge, often fished in darkness, and the other is with the mayfly spinner, fished in the late afternoon and early evening. If you are lucky this is how it can happen.

David Grayson went to the Boyne late in the day at the end of May 1995, hoping to spot one of the big fish taking an interest in the mayfly, which had been hatching for about a week. In fact green fly, the duns, were hatching and riding down the water with not a care in the world, because in general Boyne fish are not interested in them at this stage. Indeed, I have been on the river at the same time of day and seen quite big hatches of mayfly duns, but not a single trout rising. He went up the river watchfully, to a slow and relatively deep stretch, because the best fish on the Boyne usually lie in water of this character.

Some spinners began to appear, and soon after he saw a small rise, tight into the bank on his side of the river, some hundred yards upstream. He made his way to it, through bankside reeds three feet high. The Boyne in this area floods in winter, and leaves boggy land or a reedy margin when the river shrinks back towards summer level. The belt of reeds was twenty feet wide here. David walked through them, to just below the spot where he thought he had seen the fish, and waited. The trout rose again, but very near. In fact too near, and David retreated; he put an artificial spinner over the fish but it didn't respond. He quietly flattened a patch of reeds so that he could lay coils of line for a cast, and set up his salmon size net. It began to rain very heavily, so he put his rod down on the loose coils of line, and stood, hands in pockets which slowly filled with water, as the rain beat down. When it stopped, half an hour later, the fly, both duns and spinners, which had paused, appeared more thickly, and the fish rose again, producing a small delicate ring just two feet out from the bank ten yards upstream.

David's fly was a spent pattern, with very dark wings tied flat on a number ten long-shank wire, and this time the fish had it as it drifted over him the first time. It leapt out on feeling the hook, and then put its head down and swam around in tight circles, deep. It did this for ten minutes before its strength gave out, and David was able to draw it towards him. The banks here were two feet above the water, and undercut, with the near water fouled by weed and flotsam left adrift after the winter floods. But the fish was too weak to take advantage, and David, on his knees, with the rod drawn right back and the leader in the top ring, was eventually able to ease the trout over the net. It was a prime Boyne trout, brown-backed with yellow sides, twenty-three inches long and nine inches deep at the shoulders. It weighed five pounds fourteen ounces.

CHAPTER 10

The Small Loughs in Summer

Ireland is so rich in trout, sea-trout, and salmon waters that some of the minor game fishing goes unremarked – such as fishing the hill-loughs in the summer months; knowing when to take advantage of brief hatches, of mayfly or sedge, on waters hopeless for fly-fishing for the rest of the year; sea and estuary fishing for sea-trout; fishing small streams in autumn for big browns.

The most secretive, the most carefully preserved of all of these, is fishing for sea-trout in the sea. Irish sea-trout divide roughly into two groups – the big ones and the small ones. East coast rivers sometimes produce very big fish. The Dargle, a much-abused river flowing into the sea at Bray, twenty miles south of Dublin, has a run of really big sea-trout; a friend of mine took an eleven-pounder from it. The western systems, with the notable exception of Lough Currane, generally produce much smaller fish. The half pound finnock in the literature is sometimes actually much smaller than that.

The strange thing however, is that if you find the sea-trout at sea, and fish for them there, the average size increases out of all proportion. I know of several locations down the west coast, from Donegal to Clare, where friends have caught sea-trout averaging two to three pounds, an unheard-of weight in the neighbouring inland fisheries. (This pattern of fishing was, in the main, unaffected by the problems with sea-trout stocks in the mid to late 1980s because those problems were restricted to certain areas of the coast.) An unheard-of weight on rod and line that is, because netting on sea-trout loughs has established that there are far bigger sea-trout in these systems than are ever caught by the angler. Verified results from one scientifically controlled netting programme, on a minor western sea-trout lough, included fish of over eight pounds.

But sea-trout of this size can be caught in the salt. Accidentally, as by an acquaintance who got a nine-pounder from a Kerry bass strand on lugworm, or deliberately by a small band of quiet, knowledgeable fishermen, who do not publicise their catches. They fish such baits as free-lined sandeel, in specific locations, usually on a rising tide, and get numbers and weights of sea-trout that beat anything I have heard of from freshwaters in the west. It is not unusual to get five or six pound fish. They do not divulge their locations and neither will I.

Many inshore fisheries have been raped in recent years by unscrupulous netsmen, and of course these fish are caught only in areas unaffected by the blight that has annihilated some stocks.

Estuary fishing for sea-trout is more easily found. There is much of it along the west coast. Some is being developed; the Moy estuary had boats put on it in recent times and anglers fished on the drift as they would a lough. They had good catches of sea-trout of reasonable size, similar to those one would expect off a river or lough in the area. The size in estuaries can be much more variable than in inland waters. Shoals of fish seem to move up and down with the tides, feeding but not yet ready for the spawning run into freshwater, so there are many very small sea-trout in these populations. However, some estuaries in the west also produce very big fish; there was a twelve-pounder taken from one in recent years.

The best of this sport that I have had was on the Glen river in Donegal, when the fishing was controlled by Gael Linn. This is a short spate river, cutting through high open moorland to the town of Carrick, where it runs into rocky, tree-shaded pools until it discharges into a sea pool, and then the estuary proper. We fished the sea pool, each September, for a few years, and there were numbers of sea-trout around. They had two exceptional qualities. They were of a very good size, bigger than the general western average, for late summer fish, of four to eight ounces. These September trout weighed from about three quarters of a pound to over a pound. They were in prime condition and fishing for them was particularly enjoyable because their other exceptional quality was that they were easily caught during the day. We fly-fished and spun for them. Fly-fishing was tricky because the lure had to be fished very fast, much faster than in freshwater. A typical lough or river rate of retrieve brought no firm takes, but just nudges and nips. They showed often and if a lure could be got to a swirl quickly enough, a take was almost sure.

The freedom of this kind of fishing is the essence of its appeal. We rarely saw another angler. If they were about, they were trying to catch grilse from the main watercourse upstream. We had the whole sea-pool, and the estuary to ourselves. We fished up and down all day, then went back to our lodgings, a big Victorian house in the town, near the bridge over the river. It had high ceilings and a very wide staircase, and the vast inner spaces were freighted with solid mahogany furniture. The bath was an enamelled cast-iron affair, from an era when they were made to accommodate six footers like myself at full stretch. It was a balm for tired limbs after a tough day.

*   *   *

The casual angler will find that the most accessible summer brown trout fishing, (which can hardly be called wilderness fishing, but is rather fishing off the beaten track), is on the small coastal and hill loughs down the western seaboard. You do not have to book boats in advance for this, or hire boatmen, or suffer the trepidation that everyone feels when approaching a big strange lough. Permission or permits are usually easily secured, then you can go off for a day or half a day's fishing as the whim takes you. There are hundreds of these, from

North Donegal to the Beara peninsula. They are of very variable quality, and some are best enjoyed as a brief destination at the end of a summer hike with the children, on your annual holiday. They will supply unlimited numbers of little dark trout ready to hurl themselves at fly or spinner even when crashed into the lough with the vigour of youth.

There are also loughs with sufficient feeding to produce stocks of good-quality trout. Some are in splendid locations, such as Lough Anure in the Rosses area of Donegal, which lies on a plain just in from the Atlantic; it produces rising trout of good size, averaging over half-a-pound. Also in the Rosses are a number of small deep loughs with reedy banks and big trout, but this area gets quite a lot of holidaymakers, so the fishing is not always as quiet as I would like.

Some of the small western loughs are to be found inland, but lie too low in altitude to be properly called hill loughs. Tully Lough near Renvyle is one of these. There are about fifteen acres of dark, almost black water here, cupped in a bowl of high land and overlooked by Tully mountain. The banks are firm, there are some nice trout, and in summer plentiful falls of land flies can provoke good sport. You feel part of the food chain here, because the midges love a pale sweating townie, broiled to a nicety at the end of a good hike in hot weather. There is an old boat house, and an island which has historical associations, because I believe Oliver St John Gogarty (a noted Irishman of letters, and the model for Buck Mulligan in James Joyce's *Ulysses*) quartered his family in a house there in the 1920s. Gogarty's son Noll was a keen fisherman whom you would sometimes meet on Lough Beltra when the sea-trout were in.

If you are ever minded to climb any of the Twelve Bens in Connemara, and you find yourself on a summit on a clear day, look south and you will see the landscape reflecting light like a shattered mirror. The rectangle between Ballynahinch, Roundstone and Clifden is full of loughs, mostly small ones, and many of them are land-locked and do not form part of the complex of salmon and sea-trout fisheries hereabouts. The majority are fishable on a day permit (the Clifden Anglers Association is the main source), and they are well worth the effort. Those I have visited are high in the hills, with broad slopes falling into them, and even on a sunny day, crisp breezes ruffle their dark waters. The lough beds are stony, with dense stands of reeds in places. Sometimes there are boats but usually you will be fishing from the bank. They can offer surprisingly good fishing on their day, because though many lie in an area of fairly sterile bedrock, others are in pockets of limestone which offer much better feeding.

*　　*　　*

The most interesting hill-lough fishing I have had has not been for brown trout but for sea-trout. As this kind of fishing is best enjoyed if there is something fortuitous and unplanned about it, so I came upon my sea-trout lough almost by accident, some years ago before the collapse of sea-trout stocks in parts of the west. I had spent half the week being battered by a furious wind on a spate river. It was an absolute howler which screamed about my ears, and several times almost pitched me into the water when I was caught off-balance. These were really good conditions for that water, but a whole week of it on an exposed river

in a narrow valley was only for the very strong, so I was a little relieved when my three days came to an end.

I drove back to our rented house through a valley in which lay a lough notorious for water spouts. This was the only time I have seen them. The surface of the lough was lashed to a vapour, and the spout I saw rose like a column of spume, tilting this way and that before it crashed into the cliff face on the western shores.

That evening as the wind dropped we came south again, over rolling peatland, towards a gap in the mountains ten miles distant. We turned off short of the gap and bumped along a rough track. My wife was driving and I had time to watch the river running alongside the road; it was tawny with peat stain, but the level was right, and I was sure I was looking at a falling water; that was partly what I had come to see. We stopped at a pile of stones by the roadside. They formed a Neolithic monument called a wedge tomb, some four thousand years old. When I had suggested that we look at this I had also taken into account a small patch of blue on the Ordnance Survey map, just by the monument. And standing at the tomb, scanning westwards, I saw a glitter of water among the folds of rock. While my family inspected the tomb, I picked my way over bog and rock for a couple of hundred yards until I could get a good view of the little lough, which was near the road but barely visible. It was roughly kidney shaped, and the lobe nearest me was shallow, reeded in part, its water dark over a spongy bed of peat. The reeds grew out into the middle, so it was nowhere more than about three feet deep.

The other lobe looked more promising, and I decided to come back with a rod. The lough was said to hold sea-trout and a few salmon. Certainly the river was high enough to encourage fresh fish in, and the lough ought to hold reasonable stocks of sea-trout after a wet summer. Next morning, I got the necessary permission to fish, then I set out with the wind stirring the branches of the trees around our cottage and headed the car towards the high moor and the vast skies to the west.

Urban Ireland is in a twentieth century flux, with its share of the new brutalism in social life; but in old country like this the courtesies of rural Irish ways survive. I was bid good morning by a woman as I passed her bungalow, on my way to the lough. The first stretch

Summer, Lough Conn.

109

was overcut bog, used by local households to provide domestic fuel. There were several worked pits where the slanes had gone down more than half a dozen courses in extracting the slaps of black paste, like wet bricks, which were laid out to dry in the sun and would harden into fibrous blocks. The scent of peat smoke from this fuel will always be evocative of childhood to those of us brought up in rural Ireland in the 1950s and 1960s. Here and there limbs of bog oak and bog deal poked through the turf. I had to cross this soft bog, then shelves of rock, and crumbling drystone walls with ditches on the wrong side of them.

I followed the line of the tongue of water visible from the road, heading for a long bank which hid the main expanse of the lough. When I climbed it, I saw over fifty acres of visible water, under the loom of a mountain on the western shore. The only bank open to me was the one I was on, and I had about two hundred yards of clear ground there. This extended mainly to my left, ending in dense reeds, and bog too hazardous to cross. The lough was also clear to the right, but looped into the tongue which reached back towards the road and looked too shallow to fish.

The wind was rising as I hiked to the waterside, but I did not feel the force of it until I crested the ridge and my coat filled like a sail. I pulled my cap down tight and held my light rod firmly, to prevent it flying away. The lough was alive with marching whitecaps, providentially moving from left to the right, the only direction which made fishing possible in these conditions. Patches of high cloud flew overhead, pierced at intervals by a sun which glittered sharply on the waves. Sheep were huddled behind any shelter they could find. The few trees had branches permanently warped into the shape of pennants by the long winds from the Atlantic.

My first thought was that I should have brought a sinking line. My rod was a ten foot, three ounce carbon with a soft action, perfect for short-lining. I had strung a WF6F on it, but the floater is a penance in wind this strong; it develops a life of its own when a gust gets hold of it. An intermediate, or better still, a slow-sinker, because of their greater densities, would have penetrated the wind more easily. A nine foot leader was long enough, and I put up a Bibio on the dropper, with a Golden Olive on the point. The Bibio was developed for just such a situation as this; a lough in August, producing little in the way of ephemerids, but surrounded by heather bog and reeds, and nourished by their associated Diptera. In fact the Bibio was designed for sea-trout in the Burrishoole fishery, by Major Roberts, and it has been suggested that it was an imitation of a species of heather beetle.

The water fell away steeply from the shale bank into darkening amber depths, though because light penetration was so limited even four feet of water would have looked mysterious in this terrain. Casting was a matter of waiting for a lull in the blast, and rolling out the line. I was able to hang almost thirty feet of fly line on the wall of wind, just holding the rod up and letting it arc into the bank, with the dropper tripping over the waves under it. Very soon I felt plucks, and then saw splashes at the dropper, and then I pulled a dark little trout from the water like a cork from a bottle. It was a fish that looked as if it had been dipped in soot, with none of the jewelled colouring of trout from clear streams. Soon I was getting offers from these fish almost every cast, and by the time I had reached the opening into the shallows, I had landed over a dozen of them, not one more than four ounces. At the top of my 'beat' the water shelved up and became reedy and rocky as it narrowed to form a neck between the two lobes of the lough. This looked a bit more promising, and I lengthened line to put casts close to reeds, and around the big rocks on which, by now, waves were beating. The response was the same sequence of splash and pop.

A little of this goes a long way, and though it is good fun with small children, or when a bigger fish is possible, I felt I deserved more for being out, alone, on this high lough on such a wild day. A longer draw on the flies might be more attractive to sea-trout, if they were there. Whenever I have fished for them in stillwater, sea-trout have often seemed to prefer a fly retrieved at a good even pace underwater, rather than one bobbed on top. They will show at the bobbed fly but sometimes do not take it so well.

It was a real effort to get a good line out but it was possible, by finishing the casting stroke almost at the water's surface, to stretch out about fifteen yards between gusts. It had to be worked very quickly in the false casts to prevent it being blown aside on the back cast, and there was an unnerving lack of feel when a stronger gust claimed it. Then when the flies were on the water, the wind tore at the loop of line between butt ring and hand as I tried to retrieve, wrapping it around the rod, even when I shielded it with my back to the blast.

The sides of the waves had a shiver on them, and I could not make out the end of the line in their wash. I thought I felt a pluck once or twice, but there was such a rage of elements that all subtlety was lost. I fretted whether the flies were too big even in these circumstances. Sea-trout are very size sensitive, and sometimes you cannot fish too small for lough fish. I changed to a size twelve Bibio on the dropper. On about the tenth cast I got a firm take, from a fish which I played for a minute, and saw jump high above the waves, before losing it. This was a sea-trout, a bright-looking fish which surely meant there were more about. There is a huge difference between fishing speculatively, hoping that the fish are there, hoping that you are doing it right, and knowing it is so. The wind and all its maddening irritations became peripheral; my doubts resolved into a concentration, which many an angler will know, that guided the hand, eye, and tackle in a single purpose.

Casting became easier and despite the disturbances I was more sensitive to messages from the end of the line. After another few throws I had a positive take, again at the extremity of the cast, and this time I landed a lovely bright sea-trout of three quarters of a pound which had taken the Bibio. The day was vile from the point of view of fly-casting, but ideal for fishing for these shy fish from the bank. I have had my best sea-trout fishing, on loughs big or small, from boat or bank, on the wildest days.

I retired to shelter in the lee of a wall for lunch. Up here, on a high peat plateau behind a rim of mountains, there were no real windbreaks, just features which funnelled or diverted the gale. It tore at my clothes; my rod was almost levered from my hand; I did not dare open a fly box. To sit down and not have the continuous whistle of it in my ears was pure relief, but my can of beer still played eerie tunes when my mouth was not clapped to it.

The afternoon fishing was the most productive, now that I knew what to do.

111

Despite the violent gusts I reached out casts as long as I could manage and when the sea-trout took it was usually in the first few pulls of the retrieve; I rarely saw the disturbance in the surface, and sometimes was aware that I was missing the more delicate indications which sea-trout invariably give. This probably meant missed fish, since, if they are nipping at the fly a slightly quicker retrieve can then provoke a firm take. I had a second fish, of a pound, from the middle of my stretch of bank. When I went back to the thick reeds at the windward end, I put out a couple of casts, and I was almost at the point where a drystone wall came down to the lough when my left handed draw was stopped by a sudden solid weight. The fish went deep, quickly, and stayed there, holding an arc in my rod as the line whined in the wind. Then when it came up it threshed in the waves before diving into a weed-bed, but my net, at its full extension was able to dig it out. It was a good sea-trout for a lough like this, weighing over two pounds.

I took another small fish before I left, making two brace, all of them a slightly bigger stamp of fish than one would expect from such a system. But the best of it was not the numbers, it was the sense of reward for playing a hunch. Sea-trout angling on the managed fisheries will probably give more consistent sport, but it is organised sport. How good to experience from time to time rougher angling in the wilder waters, where nothing is sure, and you do not even know if the fish you seek are actually there. This is sometimes going to be disappointing, with the water wrong, the fish absent or poaching rife. That particular day all had come right. I crossed the peat hags with heavy legs and sat in the car, tired and slightly shivery after the battering from the wind. My cheeks were still glowing when later that night we ate the sea-trout, with new potatoes, a green salad, and cool Muscadet. I do not fish to eat, but a sweet-fleshed sea-trout, well earned and humanely killed, made a meal which fittingly ended that deeply satisfying day of a western summer.

Author fishing the sea-trout lough.

CHAPTER 11

Connemara Sea-Trout

There was a visceral reaction, in those anglers who knew the waters affected, to the collapse of the sea-trout stocks which occurred in many of the Connemara fisheries in the mid to late 1980s. Not just a species, but part of our angling heritage was being destroyed. Most Irish anglers have at some time fished for sea-trout, (or the white-trout as it is more commonly known in Ireland) from a drifting boat in the complex of fisheries which includes Costello and Fermoyle, Ballynahinch, Gowla, Invermore, Screebe, Kylemore and Delphi. The fishing has a special charm because it enlivens the days of summer when other fishing is difficult. Sea-trout on loughs are very sporting takers, and though often small, it was possible to make a good bag on productive days and enjoy sustained excitement from your first drift to the last one. There was always the chance of a good fish, and the odd grilse could also be expected. This angling has inspired part of the corpus of Irish angling literature, perhaps most memorably Kingsmill-Moore's *A Man May Fish*, which celebrated Casla and Delphi in particular.

This is magnificent country, from the rocky lowlands around Costello to the great ripple of the Twelve Bens, the most noble range of mountains in Ireland; they are always a moving sight because when they come into view you are in Connemara. Few of us will emulate Robert Lloyd Praeger, who in his classic book on Irish topography, *The Way That I Went*, cheerfully spoke of mastering that entire group as 'a full and satisfying day's work' (page 172): but climb just one of them and you have a view that will stay in the memory.

The Bens are constant companions on most of the loughs, especially on Lough Inagh where they rise from the western shores, and the quartzite on the bare rock of Bencorr glistens in sunshine. Fishing in this great natural theatre stores more memories than the size of the bag at the end of the day. There was no sight more melancholy in Irish angling than that of these marvellous loughs, both the grand and the intimate ones, deserted at the height of the season and all their boats drawn up on the shore, when the blight was at its worst. This is what the absence of the sea-trout meant, a whole way of fishing, in an entire region, was almost wiped out. In one or two systems that did happen, with fish counters registering less than a hundred returning sea-trout at periods when the records indicated that thousands should have been coming back. It was this kind of statistic which became the primary source of concern; the angling returns are indicative rather than statistically reliable indicators of the size and weight distribution of sea-trout populations.

There are now some signs of recovery, and many of the Connemara fisheries are well worth fishing again. The Costello fishery, which I describe later is one of these. Other waters are in convalescence, some worth fishing, some not. Lough Inagh, that great lough on the Ballynahinch system last season produced good fishing for the first time in several years, but it still has some distance to go before equalling the sport it gave in its prime.

*   *   *

I first fished Inagh in September 1984. The late summer had been dry, but for once we had timed things right because as we approached Maam Cross we could see the little streams were full with recent rain. We headed on towards Kylemore, where we had intended to fish, although after a day it was clear that substantial runs of sea-trout had not come into these loughs. I had a sea-trout on our first drift on Castle Lough and then we hardly rose a fish for the rest of the day.

That evening, Leslie Bryan and I asked around about alternatives, and a couple of fishermen staying in the same hotel said that Lough Inagh was fishing well. We had a few problems because we did not have a boat engine – they are not allowed on some of the Kylemore loughs, where we had intended to stay, and we did not know Inagh at all. This is a very big lough, perhaps five miles long by a over a mile wide at its extremities. Sea-trout and salmon lies on such loughs can be very localised and one really needs local guidance to find them; we also needed a boatman, so we made enquiries in Kylemore, and that is how we came to meet Sean Staunton.

Sean is one of a diminishing group of men whose family lives have meshed with the sporting history of the west in an intimate way. His father had been a gillie, retained to help fishermen not just on one water, but to travel with them as well, in both Ireland and Scotland. Sean had learned his craft from his father and had himself gillied widely in the west. He knew the Kylemore waters well, and he was free the next day, so he could come with us. We still had a problem in that we had not found an engine, and although we went as far as Renvyle that evening we could not locate one for hire. Sean thought that if the wind was not too bad we could manage by oars alone, with two of us rowing upwind.

The lough looked mild enough from the fishery office on the east side of Inagh the next morning. There was a good north-west breeze blowing down its length, but not enough to put a big wave on it. The forecast had not threatened high winds, so it was safe to go out, without the support of an engine. The fishing book was also encouraging; plenty of sea-trout had been taken recently, even though the lough needed to drop a bit yet to its best fishing height. It is a fact not generally known, especially on these big loughs, that water levels are as important as they are on rivers, for both salmon and sea-trout, and high water seems to unsettle fish; they do not take well until a lot of the surplus has dropped out. When the loughs did settle to a good fishing height they gave excellent angling in those years when the sea-trout ran. Western summer fish are not individually big, but the baskets of sea-trout from half a pound to perhaps two pounds, often were, and occasionally a big fish would turn up. In the early 1980s

Professor Basil Chubb got a six pound fish from one of the Ballynahinch loughs, when it should have been out of order, with the froth and flotsam of high water covering the surface.

We had a fine clinker-built boat, over eighteen feet long, though relatively narrow in the beam; it would sit well in a wave, and handle fairly comfortably when headed into the wind. The gear was stowed in the space under the bow; Leslie positioned himself next to it, and I was at the stern, on the rearmost thwart. Sean was dressed like most of the older western boatmen, casually, as if for a Sunday stroll, with a clean blue shirt, a pullover and a jacket, and a bundled waterproof in case of rain. We were in the angling uniform of the day, oil dressed cotton from head to foot, including the most distressing garment I have ever worn, dressed cotton over-trousers; a galley slave in a trireme was more comfortable than I was in this gear when the time came to row.

Sean slipped the oars onto the thole pins, and they stroked silently as their leather pads met the gunwales, easing the boat through the shallows. We headed downwind from the fishery office to the lower point of the little bay on that eastern side of the lough, and started fishing. Sean took us almost into the wash of the waves which beat on this shore. We fished with ten foot rods, quite long leaders of nearly twelve feet (at Sean's suggestion), and smaller flies than I would have chosen; my two-fly cast had a size ten and a twelve; Leslie fished three flies, all size twelves. Casting was simply a matter of rolling the line forward after working the bobbed dropper to the boat.

We soon knew that we would have been lost if we had attempted to fish here alone. We also realised that we were very lucky to be under the guidance of someone who knew the lough so well. Sean took us near some parts of the shore but ignored others; he drifted the boat straight toward certain rocks and told us to cast at them but avoided many similar ones. One inflowing stream provided good ground, and the area was fished closely. Another was completely ignored, because it flowed straight into barren deep water. An incident occurred near the beginning of the drift which put us in Sean's power for the whole day. He indicated a rock twenty-five yards downwind and said that a salmon was often taken there. Well, maybe. We have all heard the like from a good gillie, who is cajoling and encouraging by turns and employs a certain amount of 'kidology' to get his rods fishing well. We approached the rock, hope tempered by scepticism, and indeed there was a fish there. Leslie's cast on the seaward side brought a big swirl as a weighty fish moved to the fly but did not contact it, nor did it come again as we tried another drift in the vicinity. We fished with even more attention after that. Sean's massive hands worked the oars stealthily as we went before the wind down the eastern shore.

The sea-trout were being quite finicky that day, and we raised a few before we landed one. It was Leslie who rose the most, and that was because he was fishing more slowly than me, drawing his flies through the surface of the water and not bobbing them as I was. He had two in the boat by the time we decided to go in for lunch.

Following page: Sea-trout drift, Lough Glenicmurrin, Costello and Fermoyle fishery.

By this time we had drifted down a good way, and Sean suggested that we have lunch by the Corloo Beat, where the Inagh river flows out of the lough. We had special permission to spend a few hours on the beat in the absence of a tenant that day. The stone piers here, built in the last century and now weathered to a perfect sympathy with the surrounding granite, jut into the stream which links Loughs Inagh and Derryclare, the next lough down on the Ballynahinch system. A moderate cast will cover most of the width of the stream, and the water is full of promise as sea-trout and especially grilse, lie almost within arms reach. An angler fishes off these piers against the background of the grey slopes of Bencorr and Bencorrbeg, the nearest of the Twelve Bens.

When we had finished lunch, we had a few casts at the piers, and at once began to hook fish. The wind had risen and was blowing stiffly towards Derryclare, from our left to our right, so there was little finesse in our approach, but the fish did not mind. They were so keen that I hooked one as I raised the rod into position for a roll-cast. When I flicked it forward the line seemed to snag on a rock, then it shot downstream and I was playing a sea-trout. Sean was so assiduous that he landed the fish for us, and took them away to the boat. We wandered up in that direction once or twice to sneak looks at the growing catch. We had half a dozen sea-trout, from the morning and lunch sessions, when it was time to go afloat again.

Sean wanted to take us up for a drift around an island on the west of the lough, and then to a sand bar which sometimes held salmon, but as soon as we hit open water we realised that we should be lucky to do it. A big wave was now running towards us, as the wind had both strengthened and shifted a few points north so that it blew straight towards Derryclare. It took two of us, one on each oar, to move the boat upwind, and sometimes we felt as though we were making no headway at all.

I felt a new respect for the boatmen of old, who before the 1950s used to take anglers out on all the western loughs, including the biggest, Corrib and Mask and Conn, by muscle power alone. True there were usually two of them, and the boats of the time were sometimes slightly shorter than the one we were in, and narrower in the beam, but it was very weary work, and sometimes not adequately acknowledged.

There are still a few fisheries in Ireland, where, because engines are not allowed, the help of a boatman is not just a confidence-builder, but a necessity. The loughs of the Costello and Fermoyle system are all fished from boats using only oars, as are those on the Screebe loughs. On these you may sit in the bow like an Edwardian plutocrat and let a really skilled operator like Pádraig McDonagh of the Costello fishery glide the boat from lie to lie, orienting it to give you the easy cast, trimming it constantly so that you cover, and perhaps take, fish, and by his unobtrusive skills persuading you that what you catch is all your own doing. In the past, a few crusty old individuals were too easily persuaded, and when, in angling memoirs, they painted heroic versions of their own exploits, the boatmen or gillies were often ungratefully rendered by a few hasty brushstrokes as part of the background colour. One of the few accounts which gives due credit to the boatmen on these loughs is A.A. Luce's description in *Fishing and Thinking*. As he correctly says there, when you are in the hands of a competent boatman on his water, you are in a partnership, not a master-servant relationship.

These crusty characters needed careful handling, so the boatman had to have some of the ways of a diplomat. I know of at least one celebrated Irish angling writer of the past who would not share his boat with another angler, and who sometimes made life difficult for the boatman. A day out with him was regarded as a penance. So the best boatmen have learned to manage their anglers as well as their craft. Fish with Jerry, on Loughs Feeagh or Furnace at Burrishoole, and you will soon notice that the boat is usually drifted twice over good ground, with the bow and stern positions reversed the second time. He has plenty of experience of the sulks and silences that grow when one rod is not rising fish, and he has a lot of little stratagems like this to maintain a happy ship. We got to the shore after much effort, and the hardest couple of hours at the oars that I have ever experienced. But it was also the best apprenticeship on this water one could have had, in the company of that big and gentle man.

*　　*　　*

The effect of such a phenomenon as the sea-trout collapse in the west is all the more to be regretted because of the degree of individual commitment which has been made to fisheries here, a commitment which is relatively recent and of vital importance for the sporting future of the game fisheries of the entire western seaboard. Angling on the western sea-trout and salmon loughs became a valuable asset in the nineteenth century and many private sporting estates nurtured the fisheries in their control. This is clear from the Screebe system, and it is also evident on the Erriff with its salmon hatchery, and the work of the time is still visible all over the Costello and Fermoyle fishery.

After a long period of relative neglect in the middle years of this century, these fisheries are again benefiting from sustained efforts at improvement. The Inland Fisheries Trust was a catalyst for much of this effort, and the Central Fisheries Board has continued the work, notably on the Erriff.

But a really significant impulse has come from private interests. This can be seen on both the brown trout loughs and the systems which support the anadromous fish. Few concerns are as well run as Lal Faherty's angling centre at Portcarron, just outside Oughterard, where everything from boats to gillies to fishing advice is first class. Roy Pierce runs a similar service on the northern Corrib, and other centres are appearing on the western and midland loughs. It has not always been like this, and this trend is a boon for the angler; it also helps to sustain the quality of the angling on these great fisheries. Many years ago I was let out on a western lough with an old engine which would not secure to the transom properly because the disc at the end of the screw which fixed the engine mount in position was missing. The boat could not be turned, even under quarter power, without the engine working free and threatening to go over the side. After a half a day of raging at this I took the useless contraption back to the man I got it from who cheerfully told me that it had not been a problem for other customers.

The quality of boats may not actually have improved; though it is understandable that the fine clinker-built craft, such as were turned out in numbers by Philbin's boatyard of Cong, are being displaced by the more easily maintained fibre-glass hulls, I am sorry it is so. There is no more stable boat to fish from than an eighteen footer with the lapped strakes of larch. The best lough boat I ever had the use of was Paddy Kineavy's, of Dooras. It was beautifully kept, with blue sides and red decking, and showed none of its twenty years. It had been built by a man who had selected the best Scottish timbers, and then had it built by Philbin. At least you are now likely to find your boat ready and dry-bottomed, when you have been given the key, rather than half-sunk offshore, as has also happened to me. The quality of engines, the availability of lifejackets and the accuracy and availability of fishing maps are all great improvements.

Of all the southern Connemara sea-trout fisheries, Costello and Fermoyle was perhaps the most celebrated. In a good year it produced a lot of fish. Grimble's description (*Salmon Rivers of Ireland*, 1913) records annual figures of 2,000 sea-trout and 150 salmon for the lower fishery and 1,000 sea-trout and 20 salmon for the upper fishery. These are for the best years, and the sea-trout figures reflect the effect of stock enhancement programmes. Nowadays few fisheries can match historic highs, but Costello and Fermoyle did well in 1994 with about 1,000 sea-trout and over 100 salmon taken. Since these days all Connemara sea-trout must be returned alive, the sea-trout figures reflect that practice. The Costello management believe that this does not conceal significant multiple counting, and they correlate catch figures with the numbers and weight distribution of mature fish on the redds.

For a long time the fisheries constituting Costello and Fermoyle were separate. Now they are being managed in the most rational way, as one integrated system. It makes particular sense because this is a very big system with eight miles of river and over twenty loughs. The river has the proportions of a small spate river although its reactions to rain are more subtly graduated, because of the effects of the numerous loughs; there is also a sluice gate at the outflow from the biggest lough, Glenicmurrin (twelve miles in circumference), which sometimes influences the flows on the lower river. The loughs are for the most part small, and are surely the rockiest in Ireland. As the boat rides a wave it is not unusual to feel a bump under the keel, even well out from shore; the effect is more striking because if these loughs are the rockiest they also have the darkest water I have seen. Light penetration does not seem to extend more than about a foot below the surface.

The wilderness of the surroundings on this fishery is enhanced by two aspects of management. One is the low numbers of rods allocated to beats; you are often, yourself, the solitary figure in the landscape. Consider that only one boat with two anglers usually fishes Fermoyle, or that on Glenicmurrin, a big lough of hundreds of acres, there are four quarters or beats, with only two boats on each. The second is that engines are not allowed on the loughs, because their propeller shafts would shear within a few minutes if driven by inexperienced hands. The virtue of this necessity is an almost unearthly quiet, not only within the intimate folds of hills which enclose Fermoyle (about thirty acres), but also on the broad spaces of Glenicmurrin. With a skilled local gillie easing your boat over rocky shallows, and views over wild moorland, stretching as far as the eye can see, you can experience at the end of the twentieth century what the Edwardian tenant enjoyed at the beginning of it.

Evidence of Victorian and Edwardian endeavour is widespread. During a recent visit, in August of a dry year, when fishery manager Tim Moore and I

Playing a sea-trout, Lough Glenicmurrin.

broke for lunch on Glenicmurrin, we made for an island in the middle of the lough, and tied up the boat at a fine pier of massive cut stones, laid over one hundred years ago. The lunch hut, snug, whitewashed and red-roofed, with walls over two feet thick, sits on slabs of bare rock. On wild days in the past, the scents of peat smoke, grilled sea-trout, and whiskey lured many an angler to tarry here for more than the usual hour. There are numerous stone piers and butts on the loughs, and weirs and groynes on the rivers. There are also small cut-stone watchers' huts, over tiny insignificant-looking streams. These are sea-trout and salmon redds, and in Victorian and later times, men were paid to winter in these huts for eight or ten week spells during the spawning months to ensure that the fish were allowed to breed without interference. All this is evidence of a carefully managed fishery. In those times Connemara was a wild part of the country, but this was a specially protected wilderness.

Ever since I first fished Screebe, I have loved these Connemara sea-trout and salmon loughs. The fishing is very varied; you may fish from a boat, or from the Butts, solid stone piers which extend into the necks of the loughs where the main stream flows in or out, and where sea-trout and salmon lie. I have never yet failed to hook something when fishing from these, and nor did I on my first day at the Butts of Fermoyle, an extremely good stand, especially in high water, because the salmon queue there to ascend when the level is right. We did not have the best of conditions, a bright sun, no rain for months, and water temperature raised to tepid after one of the hottest summers on record. But we did have a blustery south-west wind, blowing waves up into the Butts. And on my second cast, a bright finnock dashed up to my Black Pennell, and was soon jumping about in the waves. We fished the Butts for an hour, then took a boat out on the lough, and drifted over wide areas of shallow fish-holding ground. Our gillie was Pádraig McDonagh, who In July 1995 took five grilse in an hour and twenty minutes from the Butts of Fermoyle.

Whereas Fermoyle and the other upper loughs of the system have been gouged out of a high plateau, and are all linear in shape, Glenicmurrin is a great sprawling lough, with long fingers of corrugated shoreline piercing the landscape. This is one of the great sea-trout loughs of Ireland: Grimble records 125 fish to three rods in one day about the turn of the century, and 433 fish to four rods in a week about the same time. The majority of these fish would have come from Glenicmurrin, which then was fished by only one boat (two rods). I have fished Beat Three, the south-western beat, with Pádraig again the gillie. Soon after starting we headed into a small bay and as we began to fish, Pádraig said that this was a drift which rarely let him down. He was as good as his word, because we soon had a sea-trout and rose several more before we headed for the comforts of the lunch hut. Glenicmurrin offers quite a different experience from the other loughs of south Connemara, because of its size. There are grand vistas from the lough, particularly out to the west , towards the soft outline of the Twelve Bens, and it generates a big wave when the wind blows. This is primarily a sea-trout lough, but it also produces salmon.

Glenicmurrin is the last lough on the system, and it drains into the Casla river, which is divided into four beats. The upper beats contain classic sea-trout water, their pools wide and slack, and the water deep. This kind of water, so slow that it may even tolerate the growth of reed and water lilies, which looks so dead to a newcomer to sea-trout fishing in the west, is the very best holding and taking water for these fish. Unlike other rivers in these islands, it will fish best in daylight hours, and in fact responds poorly to orthodox night fishing tactics. But give it a cloudy day and a good upstream breeze which flips up the leaves of the lily pads, and you have the makings of excellent fishing.

The lower beats contain mainly salmon water. I fished Beat One, just upstream of Costello bridge, for an afternoon in a recent year when it was packed with salmon, which had run in but stopped because of low water. They showed regularly, especially in the Cabbage Pool, a big, slow holding pool, easily covered by a single-handed rod, (a single-handed rod of about ten to eleven feet, with a number seven floater, will serve for the whole fishery in the summer months) but none of them made a mistake that afternoon. However, next day, Robert Smyth did have success here in the difficult conditions, landing a salmon of eight pounds. The lack of water that day was disappointing, because these lower river beats have produced very big fish in recent years. In 1994 a Dutch angler had a salmon of twenty-four pounds in July from the Sea Pools, the lowest beat, below Costello Bridge. A number of other salmon approaching twenty pounds have been recorded, and it seems to be a quite distinct strain of summer fish, unique to Costello. I know of nowhere else in the west which can produce summer fish of this size. These big Costello salmon are magnificent, deep-shouldered heavyweights; their impressive proportions are preserved in casts on the walls of the Fishery Office.

There is evidence in recent years of a slow revival in the spring run at Costello. In April 1994, Mrs Fitzjohn took a nine and a half pound fish from the Butts of Fermoyle, which was then earliest recorded salmon from the fishery. It was displaced in 1996 by a March springer. Tim Moore had several April fish, between twelve and fourteen pounds in 1995, and numbers were seen throughout the fishery, and recorded by the fish counters (there is a video camera, to confirm the numbers at one counter site).

None of this has happened by accident. I mentioned earlier that this system has always been carefully managed, and the recent revival can also be traced back to a management initiative in the 1980s. Roy Pierce and Dr Martin O' Grady, working with the proprietor Ralph Fitzjohn laid the foundations, and the work has continued under the direction of Fishery Manager Tim Moore. A salmon ranching scheme, similar to that at Burrishoole and Screebe, has been in place for a number of years, and this has led to increasing returns. There is a big hatchery complex at Costello which supports this effort. The imprinting of fish to the whole length of the system seems to have been successful, so that returning salmon and grilse populate all of it. Many fish captured by anglers are tagged ranched fish.

Similar work has extended to sea-trout development, using ova from brood stock at the Salmon Research Agency at Burrishoole. It is estimated that an enhancement project on the School House system has been successful to the point that the output of smolts from this system has reached optimum level, and fifty-eight per cent were from enhanced fish introduced as parr. Costello and Fermoyle seems to have been more successful than some other Connemara sea-

Unhooking a sea-trout, before returning it.

trout fisheries in reviving its stocks of fish.

This pattern of management is surely the way forward for these unique systems. Sea-trout and salmon need support to thrive these days. Actually, as is evident from the history of Costello, they have always benefited from a helping hand. The revival of sporting estates like Costello, and neighbouring Screebe, is an ideal land use for the delicate ecology of this beautiful part of Ireland.

CHAPTER 12

The Moy

Most Irish salmon are caught on bait. Fishing it can be an absorbing exercise of skill, but it can also degenerate into a repetitive chore, a basic means of extracting salmon to build a score. This is an ignoble end for a noble fish. The Moy is one of the most productive Irish salmon rivers, and the one whose topography is best suited to bait. But it was here that I learned how even in unpromising conditions fish could still be got with the fly, fished on a bubble float. This method is banned in many places, but where it is appropriate, on slow deep rivers such as the Moy, it is the only realistic method of delivering a fly. It is also far more fun than the alternatives of the spinner or the worm. I was glad of it one hot July day in the arid year of 1995.

A dry spring led into a parched summer and the holiday plans of many salmon anglers were dying on the vine. I had secured three days of prime time in the first week of July, when the grilse run should just have started, on one of the best western spate rivers. All through June I had looked at every long-range weather forecast and none had given comfort; in fact they were spot on. When I arrived for the first day of the fishing I had booked, I found a shrunken river, high skies, and no prospect of rain. There was not even a decent wind. I could fish my allocated beat, unsure whether any fresh fish had been able to struggle up, and almost certain that they would be reluctant takers in the low warm water. Alternatively I could change plans and go to the Moy.

I turned on my heel, and headed back to the rented house for a change of tackle. After another twenty miles on the road, I pulled into the Upper Clongee fishery. It was midday. I set up an eleven foot rod, with a fixed spool reel carrying ten pound test nylon. I tied in two droppers, using four turn water knots, about four feet apart, and left a long tail. To the end of the line, four feet below the lower dropper I tied a large oval bubble float. Then I made my way to the river, over the stile, and along the hard stony path.

This is one of the faster stretches of the river; in the old days, before the dredgers came, there must have been miles of water rushing in classic alternation between pool and stream, an ideal medium in which to fish the fly for grilse. Now when you first see the river, you are standing high above it, on a hard pan over the rocks and gravels of the old riverbed which were gouged out and thrown up on either side, to form embankments which are sometimes over fifteen feet high and which even the passage of two decades have not really softened. This mad drainage scheme has had little evident benefit. It might have allowed the reclamation of small parcels of some of the poorest land in Ireland, but it has despoiled almost an entire river system.

A few hundred yards below the fast water you come upon a big bend where the current slows to walking pace and the water deepens; this is the typical face of the Moy, and the kind of water from which most of its fish are taken. That day it had an angler at about ten yard intervals, which is the norm in the grilse season on the popular stretches of river. One was fly-fishing with a single-handed rod, a melancholy sight when his neighbours were mostly spinning or worming with floats. I had my eye on a spot just around the bend, where the river shallows up and there are a few nests of rocks which are good holding spots for grilse, but, as is often the case on this river, someone else had the same idea earlier, and I had to move down. I came to a spot called, I think, McCormack's Rocks, and decided to try it, for the good reason that no-one else was there.

I took out my box of shrimp flies and selected a size eight, a bright pattern, and a size ten Hairwing. The day had improved from the fishing point of view; there was good cloud cover now, and a strong downstream breeze had set in. I dragged the bubble float so as to half fill it with water, then set to work. Some people affect to despise the bubble and fly, and I did not think much of it myself before coming to the Moy. But bring one of the purists here, and let him use his single-handed or double-handed rod to reach those rocks, over forty yards away, with a strong wind on his right shoulder, and a high bank tipped with barbed wire not far behind. I have rarely felt so ridiculous as on the day when I tried to fish this stretch with a long fly rod. The shrimp brigade were highly amused.

The bubble seems to detonate when it lands, like a missile rather than an item of fishing tackle. You do not need to throw stones in, or your dog, when you want to wake up the salmon, if you have one of these in your bag.

It was about half past one when I made my first cast, which landed near the far bank. I saw no signs of fish for about half an hour, until just before two o'clock I rose one beside a rock. The bubble had landed behind it and I brought the flies into the kink of current in front of the rock, with a slow retrieve by the reel and a steady twitching of the rod-tip, which caused a little wake to form behind the bubble. The fish came to the top fly head and tail, and I felt a pluck but no more. I tried over him a few more times but he was no longer interested. So I moved down ten yards to another group of rocks on the far bank and saw that there was a nice little bay just downstream of them. I could aim my cast into this, so that on the retrieve, the flies would suddenly appear from behind the rocks, as they entered the thread of current which flowed on my side of them.

The wind, though strong, could not affect the momentum of the bubble float, so that the casts landed nicely where I intended. After about five minutes a fish took as the flies came around the rock and I fought it, a small grilse, for a minute before it slipped the hook. Ten minutes later I hooked another, and this time I played it using a lot of side strain, to encourage the grilse to stay down; I felt I had lost the earlier one because it had played too near the surface. This tactic seemed to work because after about three minutes I brought a mint-fresh grilse of three and a half pounds into the sandy shallows and netted it.

A little while later I hooked another, which also slipped the hook, and then rose a fish which swirled but did not connect. Then I hooked a fish, not where I expected to, at the rocks, but more towards the middle of the river, and to my further surprise it put its head down and charged upriver taking line as it went. Then it stopped and stayed down and would not yield, so that the wind played that eerie tune on the taut line which is always unnerving; this was not a grilse. I am pretty sure that I know what that fish was doing because I saw one do the same thing on the Munster Blackwater. A friend had hooked a ten pound fish in a fast run, four feet deep, and played it for several minutes until it began to sulk, and became almost impossible to move. I was able to wade out and in the clear water see that the fish was in fact lying at about forty-five degrees to the river bed, with his nose touching it, and using the current to hold position against the strain of the rod. Jagged side strain eventually moved it, but it was not easy. I had another three minutes of this dour behaviour, until my arm became sore from the leverage of the long rod. The fish came into the shallows a few times, then bolted away, before I could lead it to the net and see that it was a slightly coloured late spring salmon of eight and a half pounds. As I netted it a boat with anglers and a gillie on board came down river, and stopped to watch. It was now almost three o' clock. I hooked another grilse a few minutes later, and also landed this one, a four pound fish, not quite as fresh as the first.

And that was that for the day. I fished on until four o' clock but did not rise another fish, although they continued to show. By this time another group of anglers had arrived, brought up by the boat which I had seen earlier, and one or two had perched themselves on the rocks I had been fishing to, so that I had to move downstream to get a little privacy.

It had been not a typical Moy day, because even on the Moy you do not always go home with three grilse, but rather a day which had revealed the typical features of the river. I could not fish where I first wanted to because of the numbers of other anglers, but I eventually found plenty of room. The river was full of fish, and I was fortunate to come upon a group which came strongly on the take for a period. The opportunity was quite limited; within the space of an hour I raised seven fish, hooked five and landed three. Then they went off; the river died completely, but by this time I had been rumbled anyway, and company had arrived. You will rarely catch fish on the Moy without the river hearing about it quickly. Later, a few twists will be added to the tale. A few anglers saw my fish as I returned to the car. Some days later, as I was chatting to a local angler on the opposite bank, I heard that the fish had been taken on a shrimp! (Shrimp and prawn are banned on the Clongee water). It did not matter that in that low water the bubble and fly was by far the most productive method, and had been so for most of the season.

Above all, the Moy had yielded fish that day when almost any other Irish river would have sent you home with an empty bag. The river is ugly in places, crowded at times, but it is in its way the richest river in Ireland

*　　*　　*

Every river has its corps of master anglers, and the best I know on the Moy is my friend Robert Gillespie, one of the many highly skilled County Armagh anglers who can winkle salmon out of this river in any condition of light or water. Robert was for a time a professional gillie on the Mount Falcon water, and that is where I first met him. He is just about the best in the business that I have come across. He seemed to know every likely lie in the river, and he put up with ham-fistedness, my own included, from his clients, while being encouraging for the whole day. Gillying, when done well, is a subtle craft, involving as much man management as anything else, and the best gillies are pure gold; nothing, but nothing gives you the confidence on a new water, especially a salmon river, like that provided by the local expert at your shoulder. This is known in places like the USA or New Zealand, where they are paid wages appropriate to their skills, and due respect.

The angler new to the Moy, particularly, needs help because the lies on this river are not particularly obvious; one ten foot deep hole can look a lot like another. In fact many productive stretches are deep, very slow and canal-like. It is almost impossible to make guesses about holding areas because the surface gives so little away. Then when you find the fish, you need to be versatile to catch them. I think no other salmon river in Ireland, except perhaps the Munster Blackwater, requires such a range of techniques.

The slow, deep water can mean bait fishing has precedence, but whether it is a worm or a spinner or shrimp (where allowed) needs informed judgement. Usually it is a worm for coloured and high water, or fairly fresh fish; the shrimp for water from which the colour has almost cleared; and the spinner for high water with reasonable visibility. However, the fly is not just a piety on this river in the right conditions it is a deadly taking lure.

For example, in late May of a recent year, with low water, those in the know fished right in amongst the wormers and spinners, with fly. A bubble float was needed to deliver the flies, but I saw the client rod whom Robert was guiding one day lose two spring fish in the morning to flies, and later Mick Lackey had a handsome thirteen pounder (Moy springers are most beautifully shaped salmon) to the same method. Those who fished worm or spinner or shrimp had nothing.

The fly, fished conventionally with the long fly rod, is excellent on streamy high water when the grilse arrive, and often comes into its own in the dog days of August when the river is well stocked with fish which have been up for a while. The wormers or shrimpers usually plug away getting the odd fish. But Robert took me to the Drains on the Mount Falcon private water on a mid-August day, after weeks of poor returns, and took three fish on a size ten Munroe Killer, dressed on a light single wire, in the course of an afternoon; we rose about another four or five. The small fly, artfully fished, over lying salmon (Robert knew that there were good numbers of grilse here) was clearly the best method that day.

It should also be said that fly-fishing on such stretches of the Moy as the Drains is technically difficult, requiring long single and double Spey casting from the tricky banks. If you know the lies well, and can not only choose, but master, the appropriate methods, from worm to fly, then you can take more than a hundred salmon from the river each season, as Robert does.

*   *   *

The Moy is possibly the most productive salmon river in Ireland. It receives huge runs of fish. They begin in spring, a run which is showing signs of increase again.

Late summer grilse from the Moy.

When I first fished the Moy, in the early 1980s it was for its spring fish. They were relatively numerous then. A friend hooked and landed two, on worm, within a couple of hours of each other at the Lake River (the stretch of river which flows from Lough Cullin), on a shining April day with Nephin a sharp outline beyond the glittering water of Lough Cullin. They were the hardest fighting spring fish I have seen, immensely strong runners which would power away, deep, against the pull of heavy tackle. I landed one of my friend's fish and remember still that when grasping it as I lifted it from the net, my grip could hardly span its wide shoulder, which was a slab of solid muscle.

Then there were a number of good lies on the Lake River, just above the railway bridge. They were fished regularly by two brothers, rugged Mayo men with weather-beaten faces and wild grey hair. We met one of them on our way to the river one morning, as he returned, carrying over his shoulder a spring salmon held head and tail by a rope. It was a twelve pound fish, which he let fall to the ground with a slap so that we could admire its depth, its beautiful lines and its beaten silver sides. The brothers were vigorous men, then in their fifties, and fished worms with simple tackle. They used the thickest lines I have ever seen in freshwater. I always envied them their success, based on a most intimate knowledge of the river they had grown up beside. One day at The Joinings, where the Lake River meets the main stream flowing down from Swinford, one of them took pity on me and a friend. He set up our gear for worming, with the heavy lead that holds the bait deep in the Moy streams, and the big float needed to balance the lead; he tied on a size two hook and tangled a gob of three big lobworms on it. He set one of us to fish a sandy bank along which fish lay, at The Joinings itself, and placed the other a hundred yards upstream, at a bend. We were told how to steady the float as it rode down, what line to fish, and how far to fish. This gear, with a big pike float and an ounce of lead, is monstrous but the only way to fish bait at a distance in over ten feet of water. We were now Moy wormers.

The spring run was good in those days, and big fish were taken. I saw one weighing just under thirty pounds, lying in state in the deep freeze at O' Hara's Post Office, with every angler on the river passing along to view it. Like everywhere else, the spring run on the river diminished in the mid 1980s, but has revived since, and in 1996 Mike Tolan, manager of the Ridge Pool fishery, saw more fish running past the traps than for many years.

Spring fish run until May, then there is a trickle of grilse, turning into a flood of fish into the river in late June. This continues into July and gives phenomenal fishing in those months. Anglers quite often get ten fish or more in a day at this time of year, if things are right. The grilse run diminishes in high summer, though in July fresh fish are still coming in. The next main run is in September, somewhere about the middle of the month. These are five or six pound fish, and though fresh they can be quite coloured when they come into the river, if they have been in the estuary for long. Among these will be found some Black Backs, which are two-sea-winter salmon, weighing in the high teens of pounds.

The Moy drains a very large system, comprising its own headwaters above Swinford, and loughs Cullin and Conn. There are several strains of salmon in the system, which leads to a differentiation by size; the biggest fish are those grown from smolts of the upper river, and especially the Bellavary tributary. These are limestone watercourses, which produce very large smolts and, as has been observed, other things being equal the bigger the smolt, the bigger the returned fish. The fish which are progeny of spawners which use lough headwaters are of smaller size, as some of these streams are not so rich.

Of course the loughs themselves offer some salmon fishing, especially Conn. Friends of mine have often met salmon while mayfly fishing there in late May or early June. These would usually be spring fish. But sometimes they are early grilse. Leslie Bryan was out on the lough with Hughie Gillespie on a burning hot day in late May, towards the end of the 1980s. At four o' clock in the afternoon they gave up the trout fishing as a bad job and put out the troll for salmon, or whatever took a fancy to it. At six o' clock they came in with three grilse, having hooked at least six. One of the fish was so obliging as to jump into the boat. I am told that one was returned.

*   *   *

To me, the two main obstacles to enjoying the river are the physical ugliness of the water in some stretches, and the crowded banks at peak season. I have described the high banks on the Upper Clongee fishery. A lot of the middle river is like this, and when seen first by anglers whose vision of the salmon river has been formed by prime stretches of the Slaney or the Erriff it is a deeply depressing sight. The water seems so slow as to have very little movement, and so deep in parts as to be incapable of holding fish.

Give the river a chance, however, and you find that though the ugly high banks are fairly constant, at least below Ballylahan Bridge, the river actually has variations in flow and depth which you will need to observe to get the best from it. That piece of the Upper Clongee water which I described at the outset has its deep and its shallow stretches. Between Ballylahan Bridge and the first bend there is lovely water, broken into lots of fast streams by big rocks and outcrops of the river bed. With high water this fishes well for grilse in July and can be fished with the long fly rod. The water is deep at the bends but then shallows up again around the corner, where there are several groups of rocks, and fish can be got from these shallow lies. Then you move downstream to McCormack's Rocks, where the water is again fairly shallow. It gets deep again for the next few hundred yards, and to the end of this part of the fishery.

The river alternates like this down past Foxford, to the Mount Falcon water and beyond. There are many stretches (for example Paddons), where, in high summer, if the water level is right, there is sufficient flow to fish a fly nicely. Mind you, casting is difficult because the high banks are constant companions, and you really have to be a proficient Spey caster to deliver a fishable length of line. On the other hand there are reaches, like the beginning of the Mount Falcon public water, which are twelve to fifteen feet deep and full of fish but which need at least a half an ounce of lead on the line, with spinner or worm, to fish properly.

It is almost traditional now for groups from Belfast and Derry, and indeed all parts north to come down to the Moy for a weekend; I think I have heard every

131

Leslie Bryan fishing the Lake River, River Moy, in Spring.

northern accent on the river. It can get populous, especially at weekends at the height of the grilse season, though never so bad that you cannot find a corner for yourself, and you need to be philosophical and see the comical aspect of things. This is not Tulchan, and you will have a nervous breakdown if you do not adapt. I generally try to avoid weekends on the river, but I fished the Wood Pool one Saturday in September when there was an angler about every ten yards on the far bank. One of them was (illegally) fishing a shrimp, and extending his range by the novel method of walking along the bank, following his bait as it drifted down, for several hundred yards, lifting his rod over the heads of puzzled Germans and Swiss as he went. A family settled in opposite me, with deck chairs and all the paraphernalia of a seaside outing. They cast their Flying Cs (the bait of choice on the river at the time), with a vigour which sent them thunking into trees on my side from time to time. After retrieving a few of them I moved on.

That is just how it is. With the fishing so cheap and the grilse so plentiful, it is no wonder that the world and its uncle beats a path to the Moy. I could wish that more of the best stretches of river accommodated fewer anglers at a slightly more expensive rate. Such hopes are in vain; ownership disputes on this river are legion, and it will be a long time before a general river management plan, which its immense fishing resources deserve, is in place.

*   *   *

Despite all its faults the Moy is an ideal river for learning salmon behaviour. The numbers of fish there are so great, after the grilse begin to run, that patterns become evident that would not be apparent on rivers with lesser stocks.

The most striking aspect of Moy behaviour is the take. I never believed in this, a time when salmon suddenly took a fancy to your lure, until I fished the Moy. I mentioned one example of it at the beginning of this chapter, when the fish took with a will for an hour and then suddenly switched off.

Another example, in different circumstances, happened to me on the Wood Pool on a September day. The river was well stocked by then, but only a few fish had been caught up to four o' clock in the afternoon. I had hooked and lost a grilse, from a lie by the bank, at three o' clock. At quarter past four we began to pack away our tackle, because we had a long trip back to Dublin. As we finished, I noticed that two anglers at a bend down river were both into fish at the same time. We hastened to put the gear together again. By the time I was ready to cast, a rod upriver was into a fish. I put my spinner over a grilse which I had seen moving earlier in the day and he had it at almost at once. It took about three minutes to get him out. I went a hundred yards upstream to cover again some water we had fished earlier in the day. Within about a quarter of an hour I had another fish, five pounds and half a pound heavier than the first. By the time I landed him, half an hour had passed since I saw the two anglers into grilse simultaneously, and they were not taking so readily, so this time we did pack our gear and head off. In that half an hour at least ten fish were taken, more than in the many preceding hours since we had been there. This happens so often that there is no denying it, but there is no accounting for it either, as far as I can see. It does not always happen, but if it does, and you are ready for it, you can have a hectic time.

The fish seem unaffected by bankside or riverside disturbance. The banks of the Moy are very busy at the height of the season; and boats ferrying anglers to and fro are often on the move. I would have thought all the racket would have sent the fish into a wary sulk, but it does not seem to affect them. The Mount Falcon gillies often take salmon immediately after getting out of their powered craft, from water that the outboard has just churned over.

Another aspect of salmon behaviour I first saw on the Moy is the fishs' changes of preference as water levels change. I mentioned that a friend of mine had two springers in an afternoon on worm from the Lake River. Those fishing around him, spinning through the same water, had nothing. The river was falling and clearing, and must have been just right for the worm that day. Next day we returned with worm gear and did nothing at all, but a Northern angler came along at midday, fishing a shrimp at a very shallow depth below a simple wine cork. He hooked a salmon soon after starting, another ten pound fish which fought long and hard. A little later he hooked another, which we never saw. It stayed deep, running all over the broad river. At one point he got it close, but then it forged upstream, very deep, with the clutch buzzing, and took the line round a rock, where it chafed and parted. It was a good fish. Conditions had changed; the river was lower and holding much less colour; it was now favourable for shrimp fishing.

This preference of salmon for one type of bait over another is very clearly marked on the Moy. Another striking example occurred late in the season, when we had fished a length of river thoroughly with various spinners for just one small grilse each. We came to a stretch where there was a known lie in a run of water twelve feet deep under the far bank. One of us thought there might be a fresh fish there and, if so, it would be more open to an offer of a shrimp than the spinners which would have covered it many times that day. He fixed up the appropriate tackle, with a slim sliding float set to hold the bait at twelve feet and a shrimp on a big single hook. Once the tackle was set right, he cast across, and first run down the float shot away; a vigorous strike set the hook at thirty yards range and he was firmly connected to a fresh six-pounder.

*   *   *

I have described the Moy that I have mainly fished, the day ticket fishing available from the Swinford, Clongee, O' Hara's, and Mount Falcon fisheries. There are also private stretches, controlled by Mount Falcon and Charles Baker, where the rods and methods are much more closely controlled, and a gillie service is available. There is also of course the Ridge Pool Fishery which produces phenomenal numbers of grilse, especially in dry years. A rod is quite expensive here, as it is on the private fisheries named earlier, but you know that you are usually fishing over incredible numbers of fresh fish.

There is another Moy. There are stretches of river in the area of Swinford, which are shallow and varied and a delight to fish with the fly rod when the grilse are in and the water is high. You wade deep and fish small flies with the long rod in the classical manner. There is fishing too above Swinford which has received little notice because the rest of the river is so productive. There is very good trout fishing in the limestone streams which feed into the river and the estuary has a good run of sea-trout and some boat fishing for these has begun.

For most of us, the Moy which I have described, warts and all, is the river which draws us back each year because of its extraordinary productivity.

Landing a grilse on the Mount Falcon water of the Moy.

Chapter 13

Summer and Autumn Browns

Fishing for brown trout in the bigger loughs in the months of high summer has to be a very selective sport. Many of the western loughs die for several weeks after the mayfly goes. This is especially true of the Corrib, but applies in varying degrees to the other loughs. Weather has something to do with it: the high temperatures and sunny days that sometimes happen in an Irish summer are never the best for lough fishing. But this cannot be the whole story: as I shall describe, one can get reasonable sport on sunny days on some of the loughs. If you read A.A. Luce's Fishing and Thinking, (which, as I mentioned in the Mayfly chapter, you should if you ever fish the western loughs because it has some excellent chapters on them), you will notice from his records that he had good fishing on Conn, with wet-fly, in the months of July and August, and that he favoured a brighter day than some of us would now like. The seasonal explosion of fry, especially perch fry, is also put forward as a reason for the trout turning stiff, and this has some weight. Possibly eutrophication has also had an impact, as this increases food items near the lough bed, especially chironomids, which are more easily harvested than fly dispersed in the upper strata.

Fishing the dry fly on Lough Carra.

Whatever the reasons, brown trout in the big western loughs are not wholly reliable quarry during daylight hours in the hot months. The exceptions are when falls of land insects (including big falls of ants, usually red ones during the summer) bring the fish up, or when a dapped grasshopper or daddy-long-legs rouse the trout.

Evening fishing is generally more reliable, as many of the loughs will offer sedge fishing; the Green Peter is noted for provoking mass rises of fish on the midland loughs, from nightfall on July evenings into the early morning. The murrough is also a late evening fly which hatches well in the summer months, and some very big fish were taken on it on Sheelin in recent years.

For daytime fishing the choice of water is crucial at this time of year, and my preference amongst the big loughs would be Lough Carra. Carra's water is crystalline; so transparent that depth is difficult to gauge. It is the most beautiful lough in Ireland. As your boat's bow heads through its shallows the approaching lough bed seems to rise to meet you, and although you are in four or five feet of water you can see its finest detail with unusual clarity. Solitary limestone rocks loom suddenly and then disappear way under the keel. It is like moving through air.

The limestone marl-bed is the source of this wondrous clarity. It produces a high alkalinity which precipitates all solids from the water in a continuous cycle of solution. The bed has a sandy appearance in the shallows of Brownstown Harbour and much of the outer lough, and the brilliance of tropical coral in some places – like the shallows south of Rineen Point. In deeper parts (the lough is mainly shallow but has some sixty feet deep holes) a thin covering of green weed grows. Around the many islands there are depressions littered with boulders big and small, their features clearly visible in ten or fifteen feet of water. They are all pock-marked with the process of their continuous dissolution. The marl can be dangerous: island margins consist of some firm rock, and some ledges in advanced solution which are just crusts above pale treacly mulch; if your feet break through into this it can be difficult to get out.

We have usually fished Carra from Brownstown Harbour. Narrow roads surfaced in hard limestone flints approach it, and at every cross-roads there seems to be a sign pointing west announcing 'Lough Carra brown trout fishing'. The wide crescent of Brownstown Harbour has boats drawn up all around it, tethered by ropes to limestone boulders. The water is very shallow at the margins, with scattered rocks, and deepens as you look west, over swathes which ripple indigo and turquoise in breezy sunshine, to the Party mountains on the western shore.

Carra is about eight miles long and aligns north-south in two sections. Brownstown Harbour is on the eastern shore of the eastern section, which is the shallower and studded with islands from the ruin of Moore Hall in the North to the Keel river in the south. At Otter Point, mid-way along the western shore is a narrow gut, shallow and fringed by thick beds of reeds, leading to the western lough which extends north to Castleburke. This passage is tricky in low water and needs to be taken with care. There is so little draught at times that you can look back and see the clouds churned up by your boat's engine.

The middle portion of this part of the lough, from the island just north of Kilkeeran to the Black Hole (where depths reach sixty feet) is not shallow enough for good trout fishing, but the marginal waters and the rest of this section are very good. The best trout water on Carra is in the depths between roughly five and twelve feet. Deeper water does not have enough insect life to bring the fish up, and the shallower water is usually too clear to fish successfully.

The lough is famed for its mayfly fishing. It has a very good hatch, and the mayfly seem to be especially numerous, from midday to late afternoon, when the surface is calm. Then they sit, a fly to every two square metres, as far as the eye can see, their wings proud of the clear water, and their regular placement punctuated here and there by the swirl of a rising trout.

Mayfly fishing here has two phases. One is fishing to trout taking the hatching (green) fly, and the other is using the spent gnat. For the green fly, people dap the natural, use a dry artificial, or fish wet-fly. Of them all I think that wet-fly is the most productive if you get the right conditions. These are provided by a boisterous south-westerly wind. The bigger the wave the better on this lough, and it will fish in weather which would long have driven you in from the other bigger western loughs. The only really successful mayfly fishing I have had here has been in really rough weather, with the wind blowing above twenty-five miles an hour and pushing big grey waves over the lough. Tony Cains and I fished it at mayfly time some years ago for three days, and our best fishing was got on a morning when the wind blew very stiffly and the boat bobbed like a cork on the waves. The fish were up and willing, although the hatch of fly was no greater than on the previous two days, and they showed often. It was one of those times when if you saw a fish rise close, and could get the fly near him, he would have it. This is not always so on this lough where because of the clarity, the fish can be very particular. We had some lovely trout; Tony got the nicest one, a fish over two pounds, pure silver like most Carra trout, showing markings like black stripes over its back as he unhooked it.

The Spent Gnat fishing can also be very good here, although I have done little of it. In truth I have never had a really good mayfly session on Carra, much as I love to fish it then, fishing wet or dry-flies. My most interesting times there have been in high summer, when most of the western loughs are stone dead as far as trout fishing is concerned. Les and I went out with Robbie O' Grady on such a day one August. It was not looking a good day for lough fishing; there was a bit too much sun coming through the high clouds for my liking, and there was not enough wind for the wet-fly. We set up dry-fly rods, to fish a brace of flies each. I had on a small black fly, and on the point a slightly bigger sedge.

We went out of Brownstown and turned due south as soon as we had cleared the bay. We motored down past Lakeview Island and turned the boat there to drift back on the south-westerly towards the point south of Stare island. There was just enough wind to corrugate the lough surface. The method we used was simplicity itself; we cast the flies forward, let them sit for a while and repeated the sequence. It is a very leisurely way of fishing on a fine summer's day, and more relaxing than the wet-fly. We were chatting quietly when I rose the first fish, down near the little bay in the point. I was too quick with my strike, but I

still hooked it, and the line burned my fingers as contact was made. This was a small brown trout of three quarters of a pound, a wild fish, which we returned. From time to time in the past Carra has been stocked because natural recruitment is limited by the small number of its spawning streams, a problem which also affects Lough Mask. Half an hour later, still drifting down the east shore, I rose another, better, fish of one and a half pounds, and had a good scrap from it. I could see the fish for much of the time I was playing it – twisting, giving way a little, then running again – as is common on Carra; and as usual it appeared much smaller in the water than it actually was. These Carra trout often look like sea-trout just in off the surf, with that sharp contrast of bright silver and hard black markings. The only variation I have seen is in one or two bigger fish, one of which Robbie got, also in August, and which weighed five and a half pounds. It was marked like a tiger, in vivid yellow and black.

We had lunch in the little bay inside Stare Island, sheltered by thick growths of alder which line the shore here, and listening to the gentle grating of the boat's keel on the loose stones. We saw only two boats out, a change from the mayfly weeks when Carra gets crowded. We amused ourselves for a while looking at insect life on the small submerged stones. These often have a greasy fawn surface, which is dissolving rock, or else have regular patterns of holes in them. But the interest lies in the insects which cling to the undersides. Carra is phenomenally rich, in ephemerids, in sedge, and in the molluscs and shrimp which really make the fish pack on weight.

After lunch we moved across to the other side of the lough, and gradually made our way down past the Twin Islands and towards the long bay west of Castle Island. Nothing much happened until we got into the bay, where we were very fortunate to time our arrival with a rise to a small black fly. We could not get a close view of one, but they looked like land flies rather than aquatic flies. Usually during August land flies like crane flies, or grasshoppers are very effective, especially when the natural is dapped. But we had tried this in the morning and it was not as good as the artificial.

The trout rose sporadically around us, taking flies splashily from the bright rippled water. We changed to what small black patterns we had and fished them dry, casting as near to the rises as we could. Leslie got a nice fish on his artificial, and then I missed one by striking too quickly. When next I rose a fish my timing was better and I landed a lovely trout a little bigger than the morning's fish.

We had an hour of this activity before the rise died. Then we moved on, to the western half of the lough, and motored up as far as Castlecarra, though we did not rise another fish. We returned to Brownstown Harbour with a leash of fine trout between one and a half and two pounds, all taken on the dry-fly, in as leisurely a manner as is possible to get fish on these western loughs. It was not a big catch but any fish is a good one if you get it during daylight hours in the dog days of August. It is an odd thing that though I have tried just this method during a mayfly hatch, when fish are taking duns, it has not been any more successful then than the wet-fly. It seems to be a far better method on this water later in the year.

142   *   *   *

We all notice the change as summer turns to autumn. The winds feels fresher; the sun may be bright but the air is crisper; the birds move in restive flocks; the nights lengthen and become cooler and fogs are common in the chill dawns. This is the last phase of the Irish game angler's fishing year, and it can be very good. Now salmon and grilse can be caught which were stiff and sullen in warm summer rivers. Now too, the brown trout in the loughs move to the fly during the day again, and this is particularly true of the midland loughs. Both Sheelin and Ennell are open into the second week of October and some really good fishing can be found in the short days at this time of year, against the unusual background of browning reedbeds and turning leaves.

Ennell, with its sister midland loughs, has figured in almost every chapter of Irish angling literature, from the earliest nineteenth century works. Gregory Greendrake (probably nom de plume of J. Coad) was one of the first to mention them; Peard told whoppers about fishing them; G.D. Luard spent a chapter describing mayfly fishing on Ennell in Fishing Fortunes and Misfortunes; Kingsmill-Moore had just misfortune whilst fishing dry sedge there one evening (pages 74-75 of A Man May Fish); and A.R.B. Haldane had a quiet but pleasant day on a lough I believe, from the details, to have been Lough Ennell, described in By Many Waters.

The reader of these descriptions will soon notice one thing. Many of the angling writers seemed to be making a gentleman's progress from big house to big house when they fished these loughs. And the north-eastern shore of Ennell is still mostly beautifully kept parkland, with the big houses sitting snugly into the hills, above aprons of lawn which sweep down to the lough, or to copses of trees sheltering small boathouses. The eighteenth century Belvedere House, after which this lough was once named is still there and may be visited. A Gothic 'ruin' called the Jealous Wall, constructed in the grounds of the house, is also visible from the lough; this was said to have been built by an Earl of Belvedere to shut out the sight of his brother's house.

Ennell is a limestone lough, and its water in its natural state has a pellucid clarity, but Ennell was also one of the first loughs to suffer from urban pollution, in this case from the growing town of Mullingar. The problem was first observed in the early 1970s, and by the middle of that decade anglers on the lough noticed that their dipped oars would surface covered in a black slime. The lough was dying. It was tragic not just for the despoiling of a great natural resource, but also for the wastage of all the efforts of the Inland Fisheries Trust, which since the early 1950s had managed the lough very intensively, especially in removing predators and improving trout stocks. In the late 1960s Ennell was producing over five thousand trout to the rod every year. Anglers left Ennell, but after a sewage treatment plant was installed the condition of the lough began to improve, until by the early 1980s the mayfly returned, and the lough was worth fishing again.

* * *

Ennell is a lough with extensive shallows, indeed a greater percentage of shallows than any of the other midlands loughs. This is partly because arterial drainage schemes in the 1960s lowered the general level by about six feet. The northern lough, viewed from Hope's Point looks like one broad shallow, and in dry years the engine propeller will touch bottom on the way out and in, and stain the water with clouds of mud. You have to travel almost a mile southwards before you are over a ten foot depth, and trout can be taken in almost any part of the water you have covered.

This is one of the perplexing features of the fishing on Ennell. On other midland loughs, and especially on the western loughs, there are features which guide the angler as to where the trout might lie: rocky shores, reefs, islets, are all reliable starting points when you want to find fish. However, Ennell just has acres and acres of beautiful clear water over a bed of pale marl. There are some rocks, for example along the Belvedere shore; there are islets, like Goose and Gosling islet by Rinn Point; but these are the exceptions, and the greater part of the lough has a plain bed, usually clearly visible except for the very deep channel in the centre of the lough south of Rinn Point.

So to find fish one relies on seeing fly hatch, or on traditional drifts. This is a medium-sized lough by Irish standards, five miles long by two miles broad, but one may travel far to find rising trout. One day during the mayfly season I went slowly south from Hope's Point and it was not until I got into Whitebridge Bay, over two miles away, that I at last found a group of risers. Single mayfly were hatching out on a calm surface, and big trout were moving from one fly to the next, taking them with audible gulps and throwing big rings out into the lough. But I did not persuade one of these fish to look at my dry-fly, and had no sport until the wind freshened, and I began to rise trout to the wet-fly fished on the drift. I have found this to be a constant feature of my Ennell fishing. The lough looks perfect for dry-fly, but I have never done much with it there; usually I have fished it during the mayfly. But in favourable conditions the wet-fly has been very successful and I have never fished the lough without rising some fish. In this respect it is a much more hospitable place than either Sheelin or Owel, where one may spend very long days in apparently good conditions toiling just to rise a trout.

The clear water requires a specific approach. I like pale nylons for leaders. Some very reliable material can be dark, almost black, and looks very conspicuous to at least the human eye in that transparent medium. Traditional wet-fly does well here, but the flies need to be fished as far from the boat as possible, so as long a rod as one can manage, and long leaders are mandatory. Ennell fish seem to take the fly retrieved through the surface at least as often as they take the fly bobbed in traditional wet-fly style, so a longish line is advisable, and it is best delivered by roll casting, which causes much less line flash than overhead casting. Roll casting is generally a good style for these clear waters, where trout moving in the surface layers will easily be put down. The most successful flies I have ever used on Ennell have been wet sedges, in varying shades of brown, and in small sizes. These have always brought up fish, and more fish than even wet Mayflies during the mayfly weeks.

*   *   *

I went to Lough Ennell in early October 1995 with Rory Harkin, who has fished the lough for decades. A day's fishing with Rory has a certain pattern. A friend of mine experienced it when he went to buy a salmon rod at Rory's shop, and Rory invited him down to his beat on the Slaney for an afternoon to try it out. They stopped at a pub on the way down, and another on the way back, finishing at my friend's local, where he fell off the bar stool. They even did a bit of fishing in the interim. My friend did buy the rod. I am not able for much of this so I paced myself carefully when we made the first rest stop at a lovely pub just the Dublin side of Mullingar. It is built by a bridge over the canal, and was once, like most Irish pubs, a general grocery and bar. I think Rory could stop at any town in Ireland and immediately claim common acquaintance with several local people, mainly fishermen. The country is still small enough for this. Rory and the publican talked of the Sleator brothers, Larry and Chrisy, both great Lough Ennell fishermen who were among the first to recognise the return to health of the lough after many barren years. They were also great competition anglers. Rory, the Sleators, and many Irish trout anglers on the loughs, love a fishing match. I cannot abide them but I am definitely an oddity in that respect. The Irish lough trout angler is a very sociable character, and there is nothing he likes better than going out in a boat with his neighbours, giving them a start and a good beating, and then after weighing and the distribution of prizes, to spend the end of the day in a cosy fug of beer and fishing talk.

We went on to Mullingar, turning south for the lough. We passed the inflowing stream at Butler's Bridge, a rendezvous point for anglers and boatmen in the past and mentioned in some of the descriptions of Ennell. Then we eased along narrow bumpy lanes running through thick deciduous woodland until the land cleared before us, and beyond the pastures lay the lake shore. We were at Hope's Point, and Rory made a courtesy call on his friend Myles Hope, who rents boats and engines from here. Mrs Hopes vines were doing specially well in that warm year and on previous visits I had admired them in her conservatory when I had called to pay for my boat and engine. About twenty boats were drawn up at the point, and three of them were about to go out; that would be the usual number in late afternoon at this time of year. Ennell is heavily fished (some would say too heavily fished) during the mayfly season, and especially at weekends. But I have always had plenty of sea-room when I have fished here, as I usually do, in mid-week, and even at weekends at the very end of the season.

We had a good fishing day for late September. A nice south-westerly breeze blew up from the direction of Kilcooley, and grey cloud bulged down from the sky. We were spared the horrible fishing conditions that go with the Indian Summer experienced so often in recent years – cold nights, hot days and clear skies. The wind allowed us to fish drifts on the west side of the lough first, from Rocky Island, up past Dysart and on towards Burrow Hill. There was little in the way of fly life; some ephemerids, and land flies, but mostly sedge from the dense stands of reeds, now turned sepia, that fringe the shores on this side. Yet after a quiet first hour, we began to rise fish consistently, just at the point where the deeper water gives way to pale shallows. It is always surprising to see this pale ground stretch way ahead

145

of the boat, and then for a fish to flash suddenly to the flies from the apparently empty waste. As usual trout were preferring the sedge, but we were rising rather than hooking them, which is often the case late in the season.

We put in for a cup of tea at a gap in the Keoltown Reeds, dragging the boat up on the coarse sand to the bleached margins which are a feature of these limestone loughs. The bottom here crunches underfoot because it is densely covered with the shells of molluscs. We drank our tea perched on grey boulders which had the characteristic pock-markings of dissolving limestone. Eastwards the cool wind ruffled the clarity of the water to patches of blue and grey, austere in comparison with the colours of the mayfly weeks on this lough when it reflects myriad shades of green.

The fishing only got going properly after tea, and we rose a number of trout between five and nine o' clock. Most of them we did not hook. I made my usual mess of hooking a fish which took just as I was about to lift the fly from the water, not ten feet from the boat. I tried to set the hook by hauling on the line, but the rod was too far back to maintain tension and a nice two pounder went free. The fish rose beautifully to the flies, coming head and tail and showing their colours, and if they missed, coming again. I finally got one that rose like this to the bob fly just as I was lifting it to skim it to the boat, so I was able to set the hook securely, and then to lead it around the back of the boat and play it out. It was a pound and a half fish, which is the Ennell average. It was also one of the more brightly coloured ones, with plenty of black and red spots. Many of the bigger Ennell trout are silvery with pale lemon markings, and for shape and condition I think they are the finest trout I have caught in Ireland. I had one such fish during the mayfly; it was not a big fish, just slightly above average for the water at two and a quarter pounds, but it was the picture of perfection of a wild trout. You can have all your big headed cannibals, and stockfish which look as if they have been on steroids. The best trout, the most sporting fish, is still the one which rises well to the natural fly and whose lines and depth come from good natural breeding and feeding.

The fish still rose as the air got cold and the night closed in, and Rory took a good trout when it was too dark to photograph him landing it. After all the action we came in with just one trout each, but it had been a grand afternoon, and the bag would have been bigger with smarter work at our end of the line. The other boats eased in to Hope's Point in the dark, and ours was no different from the common experience, each angler having one or two takeable fish. We pulled the boats up on the rough limestone, and put away rods and reels, some of us for the last time in the season, although Ennell would continue to fish like this well into October and would provide some anglers with their best trout fishing of the year.

Chapter 14

The Late Runs

The Quarry Pool on the Munster Blackwater eddies darkly under a limestone cliff, and is fit only for fishing with spinner or worm, but there is a good length of about one hundred yards of broken holding water running down to it. Les Bryan and I had the beat to ourselves on a day in late September fifteen years ago and concentrated on fishing this run with fly. It was the final day of a week which brought the first harbingers of autumn. The night air condensed still and cold, and at Ballyduff where we were staying, the river misted the entire valley in the mornings. We would set out in warm clothes, but by midday, when the sun turned hot, we sweated our way back to the car in overheated rubber chest waders.

The Quarry is not one of the best Blackwater beats; not nearly as good for the fly as, for instance, the beautiful Ballyhooley beats, which are superb, but it is a pleasant spot. The ruin of Bridgetown Abbey, a thirteenth century Augustinian priory lies nearby and is especially evocative on a late September day when we all feel the transience of things. Just downstream is a junction pool where the Awbeg joins the main river and marks the end of the beat. This is the area described by G.D. Luard in his very literal memoirs Fishing Fortunes and Misfortunes (1942) and Fishing: Fact or Fantasy? (1947). The first volume is dedicated to R.G.A., Richard Grove Annesley, owner of Anne's Grove, a fine house on the Awbeg, where Luard stayed. The big river he describes is the Blackwater. The personal reminiscence is a bit tedious, but the books are interesting as a record of Irish fishing in the middle years of the century, not just in Munster, but also in the Midlands, and Connemara.

The weather changed that day. From noon a cool blustery wind ruffled the water and soughed in the trees; the rooks cawed and tumbled in their restive autumnal flights. When we set to work I used Leslie's Hardy Wye and a floating line. He put on a sink-tip, fishing a size eight General Practitioner. We saw a fish show at the end of the run towards the right bank, where it was holding in front of a rock, and we made pass after pass down to the lie without a hint of interest until the General Practitioner finally provoked an attack. The fish was a dark, ten pound cock and played obdurately in a swift run of smooth water for over five minutes, surging up and down with great power against the tight hoop of the rod. That was the last salmon of the season.

Ireland does not have a great autumn fishery like the Scottish Tweed. It does have good autumn runs of fish which often enter the rivers after the close of statutory seasons and head to the redds unimpeded by the lures of legitimate angling. Many east coast rivers have such runs, which may extend into November, and sometimes outnumber spring stocks.

Although the latest of these fish are of little sporting interest, the early autumn runs are a different story, providing there is water in September. (Most east coast fisheries close at the end of September). A good flood can give excellent fishing on the Nore and Suir especially, and the fish are as sizeable and handsome as springers. Les had a twelve-pounder from the Nore, on fly, at the end of September a couple of years back and it was a better fish than many caught in March or April. But these past few years the rains have not come in time, and September fishing has been frustrated by persistent high-pressure regimes which keep the Atlantic systems at bay.

The one river where you may get autumn fish in low water is of course the Moy. It is a truism of Irish salmon fishing that there is always a chance of fish on the Moy. Salmon will run into the estuary and even into the length above the weir at Ballina called the Canal, usually during the night, and may rest there, or fall back, in full daylight. If they rest you have a chance. The river is broad and very shallow in low water conditions, up to and beyond the eel traps. You can see the bottom almost everywhere and although the water looks sterile, it often holds a lot of salmon

Playing a September salmon in the Quarry Pool, Munster Blackwater.

It is a fairly scruffy bit of river but one of the few places in Ireland to offer a real chance of fish in a dry September. I have just come back from a day there with some friends. It has not rained for a month and the country is parched, but we had two fish in the morning from the Canal, one below and one above the eel traps. Although the water may be scruffy, Moy fish in this reach can be fresh and pretty even in September. My friend had a silver six-pounder, as bonny as any July fish. My four-pounder was slightly coloured, but still a grand little grilse and not to be compared with the tartan army muscling its way upriver on other systems at this time of year. We got them on size fourteen shrimp flies (which both fish had taken well down), tied by Robert Gillespie.

*   *   *

October fishing is more restricted. On the east coast it is limited to the river Fane, which flows from Lough Ross in south Armagh, past Cullaville and into the Republic, entering the sea in County Louth. The Fane is an amazing river. The year I first saw it was very dry and few salmon had run above Iniskeen. I had never been on the river, and I had arranged to meet a friend at a bridge near the water works. When I looked over the bridge parapet I was appalled. The 'river' was about thirty feet wide and a foot deep. It did not look as if it could give shelter to a decent trout.

I was taken downstream, still in a state of disbelief, following the river's course as it wound through pastures and fields of stubble, running deeper and slower. It was much more like a coarse fishery than a salmon river. John Hughes, secretary of the local club, (the river in this part is controlled by an association) would stop and point to a shadow deep down and say 'fish'. I could not have put my hand on my heart in agreement until we came to a slightly wider pool bordering a potato field. A couple of anglers were fishing from the far side. As we looked and our eyes became used to the water I at last saw fish and it was the most extraordinary sighting of salmon I have experienced anywhere. Of course it is common to see fish at Galway Weir, and the Ridge Pool on the Moy, but here, in a pool fifteen or twenty feet wide, thirty feet long, and not more than five foot deep at most, there was a shoal of about twenty salmon. Someone had thrown in potatoes from the field, and the salmon were outlined against them. They would make a little circuit of the pool now and again, allowing us to pick out two really good fish, one of them was at least fifteen pounds.

The anglers were using shrimp (bait is permitted on the river) which we could discern as they drifted down to and past the fish without stirring a fin. We came upon anglers all the way down, fishing tiny pools sheltered by trees which grew all along the banks. Some of them had fish by this time, midday, and one man had two. All were reasonably fresh-looking salmon for the first week in October, weighing between four and eight pounds. It was the more surprising because the weather was completely against sport: there had been little rain for weeks and that day was typical of the previous month, clear, bright and windless. But by the end of the day that part of the Fane had yielded over twenty fish.

I did not see the Fane at its best. With good water the fish run right up into the northern sections and give fishing all the way. Good water requires a lot of

149

rain especially after a dry spell, because the feeder loughs must first fill, then spill over before the river gets a proper flood along all its course, and although it may be narrow and relatively shallow it produces well to the fly when there is sufficient volume to put a proper run on the streams; there are some lovely stretches which respond well to the fly.

All Irish rivers, and especially east coast rivers need close protection to safeguard their stocks. Some fine rivers have gone into steep decline and are hardly worth fishing any more. This doesn't happen on the Fane. It is one of the best managed and protected fisheries in the country, for which clubs like the Drogheda Angler's Association are responsible. The Fane's season in the Republic ends on 12 October, and that is the effective end of the salmon season on the river in all but exceptionally wet years.

*   *   *

The latest autumn fishing is found on rivers like the Faughan and the Roe, in County Derry, both of which close on the 20 October. These rivers benefit from the huge runs of the Foyle system but are marked by the fact that their stocks are mainly late ones. The Faughan gets its first substantial numbers of fish in July; the Roe's main run comes later, towards August and September. The Faughan's numbers can be assessed by totals from the fish counter at Campsie Dam: in late September 1996 over seven thousand fish had already run through and more were expected; and this may have been an underestimate as the counter is thought to detect only fish above four pounds. There is no fish counter yet on the Roe system, but it is estimated that the total take of rod-caught salmon probably exceeds two thousand fish a year, which is similar to that of the Faughan. Besides the late run of salmon the Faughan is also an excellent sea-trout fishery, particularly in June and July when bags of twenty or thirty fish a night have been taken by anglers who know where to go. These sea-trout would run from about one pound (the average size) to three pounds.

Late salmon on both of these rivers are sizeable fish. Take one I saw on a recent September day, caught by Alastair Leslie fishing the Faughan at Lynch's, above Campsie Dam. It was a coloured but splendidly shaped ten-pounder, short and deep and thick across the back. Curiously, he said that such fish were from introduced stock, and that the true Faughan fish was a longer and slimmer specimen. This stamp of fish is the norm rather than the exception on these rivers in late season. They may be spotted at any time swimming around in the shallow water at low tide below Campsie Dam, in the sanctuary area.

The Roe and the Faughan are spate rivers which ordinarily would drop to bare bones very quickly, especially with the assisted run-off caused by drainage schemes in recent decades. They twist in narrow muscular courses through steep valleys. The Roe has even cut a deep and shaded gorge (in the park area) where the water volleys from rock to rock in the sharper gradients. The Faughan runs down very quickly, and a heavy flood will give only a day's fishing on falling water, if that; a similar flood on the Roe might provide a few days of high-water fishing.

However, these valleys have features of industrial archaeology not found in similar rivers in the south. Disused mill buildings, and associated weirs, stand all along both rivers. There is a mill on the upper Faughan only three miles below its source, and numerous others at regular intervals downstream. Most are now disused, as they were associated with the flax industry which thrived in the nineteenth century but failed in the mid 1950s. All these weirs, with their laydes (a local name for the mill leat, which diverted water to the mill wheels) impound the streams and provide pools where fish may be sought even in low water. The most prominent of these works is still functional – Campsie Dam, built to impound water which could be diverted to the Cortauld site. The impounded water backs up almost all the way to Mobuoy Bridge and provides deep pools, the Clay Hole, the Sand Hole, and others, which shelter fish. The salmon which I mentioned earlier, taken by Alastair Leslie on a small fly (I did not see the pattern) was caught despite no rain having fallen for a month.

Alastair got the fish because he is one of the expert local rods. He knows that stretch like the back of his hand and would get over forty fish a season from it. He has adapted his tackle to cope with the terrain. The banks are treed and sometimes high above the water line. Hooked fish may run far; the one I mentioned ran around a corner. He uses tackle which might seem heavy at first sight, especially his rod, which is over sixteen feet long, but it is a good choice for this length. We watched him place his flies (most anglers on this river use fly, and almost all use a dropper) delicately and at just the right angle in a difficult bend of the river. The long rod allowed him to lift the back cast above the bankside trees and rough growth. It could also reach out to control a heavy fish motoring up and down the narrow river.

*   *   *

These rivers can only be understood in terms of their intensely local character. Their distinctive terrain and archaeology is one aspect of it. An almost fierce personal attachment on the part of their anglers is another. Derry anglers are generally Faughan men. The Roe, which flows through Limavady, is largely fished by anglers from that town. Allegiance is actually even more specific, because some anglers only fish certain pools, or stretches of the river (almost every inch of each river is named) and come to know them as well as a fond gardener would know his plot. They are not entirely pleased to see another rod on their pitch, and in the matter of accuracy of returns, they are canny. A Faughan angler might be happy to tell you that he had enjoyed a good day, but a little reluctant to say at exactly what spot, and using which fly, and just how good a day it was.

This presents some difficulties to the local clubs. Both the Faughan and the Roe are very well-managed. Almost all angling on the Faughan is controlled by the River Faughan Angling Association, a limited company, which guards its waters with jealous care and retains two full-time bailiffs, as well as honorary bailiffs to ensure the well-being of its stocks. However, it seems to be difficult to get accurate returns out of the man reluctant to give too much away; the total return is estimated to be about sixteen per cent of the true figure, so catch details have to be extrapolated from this.

The loyalties are described in some excellent books written by local men about each river. I know E.C. Heaney's Fly fishing for Trout and Salmon on the Faughan (1947) only by its local esteem. But I have read and enjoyed the late Olly McGilloway's Along the Faughan Side, (1986) and Conly George's Reflections and Ripples (1983). Ollie McGilloway's book is a very fond description of the Faughan, detailing almost every pool from source to mouth; it is required reading for a stranger to the river. The visiting angler would also profit by reading Conly George's book before he wet a line in the Roe. It is pamphlet-sized and less detailed than McGilloway's, but speaks with an authentic local voice and gives the outsider a feeling for the emotional attachment of the Roe angler to his river.

The attachment is easily understood; this is a beautiful water. I was first guided along it by my friend Tommy Simpson, who has fished the river since he was six and has taken over a hundred salmon from it. On that day we parked near the old flax mill at Carrick, and passed the flax retting tanks, and the tall brick chimney, on our way to the Alder Pool. After that we fished Givens Weir; the Knowes Pool, then shallow in low water but still holding fish as Robert McHaffie, a master local fly-tier had taken a ten-pounder from it the previous evening; and Carrick Flats, some hundreds of yards of flat water between two weirs, littered with rocks and a great holding pool. For the afternoon we concentrated on Carrick Rocks. You reach it by a rough walk upstream from the top weir at Carrick Flats, or by taking the steep flights of steps down the gorge which the river has cut here. A pretty little church, in weathered grey stone, overlooks the river. Although the water was low it still flowed quickly enough to allow us to fish the fly, and the midday sun was dimmed and filtered green by the time it had penetrated to the depths of the gorge. We made our way downstream, spey-casting left handed into the runs which bounced from rock to rock. Some of the rocks were huge boulders of several tons weight. Although we did not rise a fish we saw several, including at least two in a lie just above the footbridge. We fished worm over these for the last couple of hours. On this river the worm is fished freeline, or freighted with a little lead in heavy water. We did not need lead in the low flows, so a couple of worms provided enough casting weight. As the worms passed through the lie, which was the space from the far side of a submerged mid-stream rock to another rock five yards below, occasionally a fish could be seen to turn, or its sides to flash. Once, as I retrieved the worm at the end of its drift it was followed up by a heavy salmon swimming only a foot behind. It was the nearest we came to catching one that day.

* * *

The length of their tidal stretches greatly increases the chances of sport on both of these rivers. The Faughan is tidal as far as Campsie Dam. The Roe is tidal almost as far upstream as Limavady, a distance of nearly five miles. The value of sport in tidal waters is sometimes underestimated on salmon rivers, where the state of the classic pools is the limit of many anglers concern. But tidal fishing is good even in low water as long as fish are coming into the system, and in the climactic regimes experienced at the beginning of the 1990s, when Septembers and Octobers have sometimes been unseasonably dry, the tides have stimulated the only sport with fresh fish on these late rivers. Salmon move up and down on tides, even when there is little fresh water coming down. They also will lie in some areas of tidal stretches.

The fishing is generally best from about an hour or so into the ebb tide to low water, and then for about the first hour of the flood. On my first visit to the Faughan, I went to the offices of the River Faughan Angling Association, in Carlisle Street in Derry, and Lance Thomson issued my ticket and gave me some fishing information quickly before urging me to get to the river as smartly as possible because the ebb was just about to begin and that would offer the best chance of a fish in the low water conditions then prevailing. Timing is extremely important on these tidal reaches, and you will find that the local anglers are acutely aware of it. Tommy Simpson took me to a tidal stretch of the Roe one

Landing a fish taken on worm, River Moy, September.

morning, a little early because the level was so high that the tops of the posts buttressing the riverbanks were still covered. We had the river to ourselves and went for a walk downstream before returning to the pools we intended to fish. By the time we had come back, and the water had fallen to a nice fishing level, we met angler after angler who had appeared as if by magic.

The first portion of the ebb is poor partly because a lot of flotsam is carried back down and the water can be dirty. The first hour of the flood, although sometimes good, can also be spoiled by dirty water. I was fishing the Faughan just below the Drain on a flood tide which began to run at dusk, often a coincidence which can produce a fish, but on this occasion it was spoilt by clouds of silt stirred up by the strength of the flood, and a lot of floating rubbish. Running fish were showing but the water was too dirty to fish for them. The tide that evening was going to be a big one and that produced too heavy a surge for fishing the flood stage.

The tidal fishing on the Faughan is mainly from the banks. On the Roe because of the greater length of tidal water, the best fishing is got on the ebb when the water drops sufficiently to allow one to wade in some of the lower pools, then the fishing is just like that on a classic pool. Most anglers use fly, and a single-handed rod or a short double hander is sufficient. The river is only thirty yards wide at most, and the fishing is both comfortable, for the wading on small gravels is ideal, and delicate.

A good stir can come on the fish as the tide ebbs, even when the upper river is stale from want of fresh water, but for this a cloudy day with a fresh breeze and a little mizzle is needed. That day when Tommy was showing me the river was just so, and the fish began to roll and move as the water fell. By the time it had dropped three feet sport began, and Tommy netted a resident cock fish of about seven pounds for an angler. Then he rose a salmon himself, and hooked and lost a silver fish of about ten pounds, which had not long moved in from the sea. This good sport continued until the turn of the tide.

*   *   *

Tommy hooked his fish on a red shrimp fly. Conly George, writing about his experiences when beginning to fly-fish for salmon on the Roe almost fifty years earlier, in 1948, refers (on page 50 of his book) to only two patterns, the Roe Purple and the Curry's Red Shrimp (a fly devised by the late Pat Curry of Coleraine). The local faithfulness to shrimp patterns is one of the lines of continuity in salmon fishing on the Foyle system. In fact, this is the land of the shrimp fly and if you fish any of the Foyle rivers, at any time of year, you will find that the specific medicine for the most difficult fish is some variation of shrimp pattern. This applies from the earliest spring days on the Finn or Mourne when dressings on hooks as big as size fours are used, to these first weeks of October.

The spread of the shrimp fly seems to have happened relatively recently. Stuart Donaghy, a fourth generation Faughan angler who contributed a chapter on salmon fishing to Ollie McGilloway's book asserts that: 'There have been vast changes in the pattern of salmon flies during the past 25 years, more perhaps than occurred during the previous 100 years. About 25 years ago all but a few flies, used in salmon fishing, were winged patterns, and the majority used on the Faughan had bronze mallard as the winging material.' A similar view emerges from Robert McHaffie, writing about E.C. Heaney's flies for the Faughan in Trout and Salmon in July 1987; these flies would have been in use up to the 1940s. The salmon patterns illustrated there are all dressed on single hooks and include the Dirty Olive and the Major's Red, both using seals' fur for bodies and mallard for wings. I think that McHaffie's Major's Red is the same fly as Donaghy's Fiery Brown variant, which had a dark blood red body as tied by Major McConachie. A tentative conclusion from this is that up to about the 1940s, Faughan and Roe salmon flies were conventional winged patterns.

Donaghy believes that the origin of the shrimp style of tying can be traced to Hardy's Wye Bug, although there is evidently local difference of opinion about this. There can be little doubt about the popularity of two patterns, the Faughan Purple, and Curry's Red Shrimp, or variants known simply as Red Shrimps. A point to note here is that it seems the colours purple and red were specially favoured in these Derry rivers before shrimp flies were developed. Here is Donaghy again: 'the Faughan Purple [is] so well known here, as a salmon fly, that the colour of the purple used to be a source of debate amongst anglers and the secret of the correct dye was something that was only passed from father to son'. And as for red: 'my own preference was for the red shade [a dark blood red shade of body wool for the Fiery Brown] and for many years it was my point fly accounting for many salmon'. The secrets and conspiracies and suspicions about specific colours in patterns continue to this day and there are anglers on the Faughan and Roe who will never let you see their fly, or who will bind you to secrecy if they do. There is something almost Masonic about the fly-tying traditions in this part of Ulster.

The aspects of both pattern and size are significant. The Foyle tradition of using relatively large flies applies here, and you will commonly find dressings on size eight hooks; sometimes size six and even size four trebles might be used in heavy water. These are very large hooks when compared to the sizes used in other parts of Ireland, where the tendency has been for the use of smaller and smaller flies as modern patterns for the predominant grilse runs of recent decades have evolved. This influence is beginning to be seen on the Faughan, but generally anglers on these rivers use larger flies than their brethren on other systems.

Shrimp flies have had a liberating influence on the Irish fly-fisher. For too long the orthodoxies from big, classic Scottish rivers concealed the full effectiveness of the fly on Irish waters. When we used flies from, say, the greased line series, Hairy Marys, Blue Charms etc., we did as we were told and fished them on slow downstream drifts. However, when we put on shrimp type flies we felt we could do what we liked and we pulled and jiggled them as they came around the currents; when we fished them in flat or dead water we relied entirely on hand pulls to give them life; we fished them upstream and across and downstream; we learned to forget about letting them drift at the same rate as the current speed and instead experimented at fishing them at varying speeds. On some southern rivers shrimp flies are fished with a bubble float and fixed spool reel where delivery by long rod and fly line is not possible. This is done mainly on the Moy, and here I have learned from my friend Robert Gillespie that in lowish water the fly will outfish anything else, as long as you have the right fly, from about May to the season's end. I have seen fish taken on fly in almost every month, when the wormers and spinners and prawners, fishing the same water, have gone empty-handed. I gave an instance earlier, when two of us had fish on Robert's little shrimp pattern while other anglers on the same reach using all methods, took nothing. I am not saying fish will always prefer fly: I am saying that when they have seen everything else, then the right fly will be as good as anything, and better than most. We got our fish that day by casting directly upstream in rippled water and retrieving fairly slowly but still faster than by hand. And the fish took the flies as confidently as possible.

The season really ends for me on about the last Friday in November, when our little group meet at Leslie's to share a goose, some nice wines, and to swap fantastic and unreliable yarns about the season just past. I should say now that I tie my stock of shrimp and other flies in the winter months, and encourage others

to do the same, but it is not true. I rarely get around to tying much in winter, rather, I do it hurriedly during the season, acting on the stimulus of some new pattern or material or incident. What I do in winter is to read some of the old books again and plan my trips for the next season. Perhaps plan is too formal a description, because there is as much daydreaming as planning involved, and I never get around to fishing all the places I have in mind. It would not be possible in Ireland unless one were a full-time angler.

That fills time in December which is a grisly month for the Irish trout and salmon angler. In January, the early salmon rivers open again, and the hardy annuals are lined up at Islandbridge in one of the great displays of faith, trying for a Liffey salmon. Spring is only a month or so away. Why wouldn't the Irish game fisherman be a happy fisherman?

October salmon from the Fane.

INDEX